President Nixon's

Psychiatric

Profile

President Nixon's Psychiatric Profile

A Psychodynamic-Genetic Interpretation

by Eli S. Chesen, M.D.

Peter H. Wyden/Publisher
New York

LIBRARY OF CONGRESS CATALOG CARD NUMBER: 73–90919

MANUFACTURED IN THE UNITED STATES OF AMERICA

ISBN: 0–88326–069–7

To the patience of
my parents,
Peggy,
and a gifted teacher, Lee Cohn.

Acknowledgments

I would like to give credit to Leon Salzman, M.D., whose writings have served as an inspiration and partial foundation for this book. Similarly, I want to express gratitude to Hugo L. Cozzi, M.D., for his aid in clarifying for me many of the principles described herein. I am especially indebted to Louis L. Bruno, M.D., my "Ivy League alter ego," for his honest criticism, suggestions, and encouragements. I am deeply appreciative of Richard McC. Shannon, L.L.B., for his criticisms and political-legal perspectives on the subject. Likewise, I want to thank Ms. Jeannie Shannon for her perspectives and encouragement. I am also grateful for the efforts of Peter H. Wyden for his part in making this manuscript as readable as it is. I must also acknowledge the news media for making possible much of my own direct research, especially the Public Broadcasting System for its faithful coverage of recent news events.

I am most of all grateful to my wife, Peggy, whose endless researching and manuscript preparation has augmented my credibility and clarity. And thank you, Chelsea Lynn, for your patience.

Contents

1

*Why This Profile
Is Necessary and
Possible*

The caucus room, where Hiss had appeared three weeks before, was again jammed. Klieg lights and television cameras were set up for the first major congressional hearing ever to be televised. It was unfortunate that, back in 1948, there were so few television sets in American homes. Had millions of Americans seen Hiss on the stand that day—as was the case, for example, when Estes Kefauver questioned Frank Costello in 1951—there would not have been the lingering doubts over the Hiss case which have continued for so many years.

—Richard M. Nixon, *Six Crises*

**TV as an ana-
lytic tool**

In this reference to the Alger Hiss case, which in 1948 made "Richard M. Nixon" a household name, Nixon implies that people—"millions of Americans"—can make intelligent and serious judgments about other people simply by watching them testify on television. I agree with him. In fact, much of this book rests on this premise.

It has been the habit of the United States government, through some of its agencies, to compile psychiatric profiles of its foreign enemies and, at times, of its own citizenry. During World War II psychoanalytic studies of Adolf Hitler were carried out, in absentia, by our government as well as others. A recent book, *The Mind of Adolf Hitler,* describes one of these studies in extensive detail. Even more recently, it was disclosed by top government officials that numerous such psychiatric profiles have been compiled on an extensive variety of people, including civil rights leaders, politicians, antiwar radicals, activists in general, and, of course, known or suspected criminals.

**1984 has
arrived**

Patently apparent is the fact that various governmental authorities, including the FBI, the CIA, and the Executive Branch, have compiled staggering amounts of sophisticated psychological intelligence on particular segments of the population. Similar profiles are gathered by the Internal Revenue Service and the military. The age of George Orwell's *1984* seems truly to be at hand.

When people refer to the Constitution, they are always intrigued by its timelessness. More specifically, they are impressed because the Constitution takes into account developments that had not yet emerged as problematic when it was written. But in the case of at least one sobering danger, our forefathers may have been myopic: Nothing was provided in our system of checks and balances to deal with the gathering of psychological intelligence. Yet our forefathers cannot really be blamed, for no one can effectively check or balance something that has been produced in strict secrecy under a cloak of "national security," Nixon's rationale for intelligence gathering. My question is: Who moderates such governmental intelligence gathering and makes certain that it is not abused? The answer would probably be less than reassuring; in any event, it has not been forthcoming.

The profiles in this book are not secret, and for the most part were compiled in my own living room as I watched my own television set,

The investigators need to be investigated

using methods that are completely open to question and scrutiny. Public necessity dictates that this be done: It is imperative that we gain insight into the minds that have not only been governing us but investigating some of us.

My intention is not revenge, but rather to answer some of the unanswered questions that have been raised by members of the public and press in the wake of Watergate and other recent scandals. Most of these interrogatives begin with "why." My answers will at times be simple and at other times complex and/or depressing. I hope they will not seem overly glib, confusing, or cynical.

Where the answers come from

Of great importance, I believe, is my detailed account of the personality development of Steve Cleansman. He is a fictional character, but I believe he is a helpful psychological device. And as you become acquainted with him, you may begin to resent as well as empathize with Richard Nixon and his closest associates. Such ambivalent feelings probably reflect your own humanism.

Once you appreciate the psychology of Steve Cleansman, the ultimate explanations of Watergate and related phenomena will become more evident, even obvious.

Perhaps the greatest irony is that the need for

my profiles has grown out of the government's obsession with profiles of its own. While there is nothing illegal per se about compiling such dossiers in absentia, the government has been unable to limit itself to this degree of intrusion. Its insatiable hunger for total knowledge led to dissatisfaction over its merely theoretical personality outline of Daniel Ellsberg—and then on to a remarkable blunder, the burglarizing of Ellsberg's psychiatrist's office.

The hunger for total knowledge

This governmental preoccupation with the mental status of people in sensitive positions necessarily triggers a counter-curiosity. What about the motivations and mental status of our governmental leaders and the figures who surround them? The public's curiosity was well demonstrated during Senator Thomas Eagleton's brief, tragic tenure as Vice-Presidential candidate. If in 1936 the German people had displayed a similar degree of curiosity about their leaders, the course of history might have been changed for the better. The fact that they did not is important and understandable, as I will show.

A psychiatric profile might well be resented as an invasion of privacy. It can also be taken as a compliment. In the unlikely event that someone were to publish my own psychiatric

Studying Nixon as a patient

profile, I could not help but construe this effort to be a reflection of the importance I must represent to him. Conceivably, I might be gratified to discover that the government was so interested in my mental workings that it would resort to profiling, burglary, and bribery to decipher them. And so perhaps my psychodynamic-genetic interpretations will be viewed by its subjects as humble flattery.

My subjects are all well-known people, and I have depended at times on some of the general knowledge about them which is available through the media. But my most rewarding source of research was not secondhand biographical material prepared by other writers and theorists. *I have studied Nixon and his associates as patients;* my television set served me well as a surrogate for opportunities not otherwise available to me or anyone else. I have spent literally hundreds of hours observing Richard Nixon, John Ehrlichman, John W. Dean, III, John Mitchell, H. R. Haldeman, James McCord, Bernard L. Barker, Herbert Kalmbach, L. Patrick Gray, and Richard Kleindienst, as well as others, such as Spiro Agnew and Billy Graham. The last can be thought of as a latter-day saint, and his association with the Nixon administration is important confirmation of the Nixon personality profile.

I have taken meticulous pains to listen carefully to the words of all these men and to watch for displays of emotion—or lack of emotion. Patterns of dress, use of humor, candor, and general attitude were scrutinized most carefully. When possible, the psychological defense mechanisms utilized by my subjects were monitored and recorded. The gavel-to-gavel televised coverage of the Senate Select Hearings on Campaign Practices gave the psychiatrist an unprecedented opportunity to examine and gain insight into the mental workings of the men who have administered our government and contributed to the corruption of our political process. A book of this kind could not have been initiated prior to the summer of 1973. Now is the time for that season to close, and the time for me to open.

Why this study was not feasible until now

From the outset, an inevitable credibility problem must be dealt with. With considerable validity, one might ask how I can expect to undertake psychological examinations of people I have never met. Some will accuse me of being overly ambitious—even grandiose.

Ideally, to perform a wholly adequate psychiatric examination on a subject, that person must meet on a one-to-one basis with his examiner. In this way a physical examination can first be performed to rule out organic pathology that might be affecting brain function and therefore behavior. In this intimate setting the examiner can also ask specific questions in an atmosphere that promotes frankness, openness, and security. And the examiner can observe the subject's reactions to his (the examiner's) questions and personality. In general, then, and given ideal circumstances, the examiner can exercise a significant amount of control over the situation.

The physician's way of observing

Yet laymen are often surprised to discover how much can be learned about a person without his cooperation—and I am *not* referring to covert intelligence-gathering techniques such as wiretapping and mail surveillance. As a mere spectator, a physician can make assumptions about people and quite often be on target. By observing only a patient's gait, a physician can suspect the presence of acute gonorrhea in a woman, or of advanced syphilis, rheumatoid arthritis, and other neurological diseases too numerous to list. It really does not matter whether the person is a hospitalized patient walking across an examining room or simply a man in the park taking a Sunday afternoon stroll. Similarly, the appearance of a person's skin can indicate blood disease, liver disease, allergies, etc. An alert internist may suspect diabetes in a person just by smelling his breath or watching him at a water fountain. Likewise, a psychiatrist with his medical and psychological knowledge is finely tuned to interpret an almost endless variety of phenomena about a person, especially from what that person says, how and why he says it, and how he appears as he says it.

Paradoxical as it seems, frequently more can be learned about someone's inner workings when the examiner is an interested spectator or observer rather than a prying interrogator. Often, more uncontaminated data can be obtained from a person under examination if the examiner restrains himself, not inhibiting the patient with questions. Likewise, much can be learned about someone just by looking at him, listening to him, looking at his accomplishments, and reading his writings.°

Questioning does not always help

My opening quotation, from Richard Nixon's *Six Crises*, seems to support this, not only for the psychiatrist but for the perceptive layman

---

°The sophisticated reader of my last book, *Religion May Be Hazardous to Your Health*, will certainly have gained significant insights into my own personality.

as well. Nixon is saying that "millions of Americans" can make valid judgments by analyzing the facial expressions and words of a man being televised. In other words, not only can a psychiatrist glean insights by observing someone on television, but so can the layman, as Nixon himself says.

Nixon: a victim of his personality

We can know much more than we do about Richard Nixon and his fan club. We need only look closely at the subtle but revealing aspects of these men to discover what makes them run. One early surmise that I can offer is that they run rapidly and powerfully, like a well-tuned Ferrari, but the fuel is not high-octane gasoline—it is *anxiety*.

More than any other factor, the neurotic need, shared by many people, to deny his own human limitations has led to Richard Nixon's successes as well as to his failures. It has perverted the political process and given us the Watergate phenomenon.

Richard Nixon made it all possible and even inevitable by serving as a rigid mold for his followers. He is a victim of his own inflexible, predictable personality. He takes himself and the intrinsic office of the Presidency too seriously—thereby showing, among other things, that he lacks one of the redeeming attributes of his one-time mentor, Dwight D.

Eisenhower. While Ike was constantly chided in the press for his self-indulgence on the golf course, part of his greatness may have been revealed by his divided loyalties (the White House versus the golf course). He realized something that Richard Nixon cannot realize.

Eisenhower knew that he was only part of the country; Nixon sees the country as *part of him*, an extension of himself. Perhaps he even sees the world and the universe as extensions of his own omnipotent being. It is no wonder, then, that many of his closest associates have seen themselves as mere appendages of the President, even at the expense of their own personal integrities.

The country is an extension of himself

At times Nixon seems to have some inkling of this distorted view of himself. In *Six Crises* Nixon has this to say about a mishap during his 1952 whistle-stop California campaign for the Vice-Presidency:

"The train started to pull out of the station before I finished my speech. . . . I had an exaggerated idea of what I had planned to say if only a mistake hadn't been made in starting the train ahead of time. . . . I laughed and recognized that I had just experienced another example of the truth of one of Eisenhower's favorite admonitions, 'Always take your job, but never yourself, seriously.' "

Unfortunately, President Nixon's personality characteristics have seldom allowed him to accept and act upon Eisenhower's advice (or anyone else's) to any great extent.

Why did it all happen?   Analyses of Watergate and related phenomena have dealt mostly with the effects of what happened. I am more concerned with cause than effect. As a psychiatrist, I am not searching for blame. Nor do I wish to hypothesize as to who knew what and did it when. Rather, I am analyzing personality structures in search of patterns. I believe I have found a pattern, and within that pattern I have found some reasons, causes, and answers to the puzzle plaguing us: Why? Why did it all happen?

Before proceeding to assemble the puzzle, the pieces must be found and identified. In the following chapters I shall first identify and examine some of the pieces of this human puzzle. As with any incomplete and very complex puzzle, a bit of patience is required; some of my pieces will not fall into place at once.

I was once advised by one of my teachers, a well-known psychoanalyst, that psychiatrists should keep their noses out of politics and other public affairs and confine their skills and energies to the diagnosis and treatment of mental illness. I must humbly but vigorously depart from such advice. Nor do I believe that other medical specialists should function only as technicians.

The gynecologist knows that he can all but eradicate cervical cancer if he can encourage women to have regular pelvic examinations and Pap smears. I think it is his business to actively promote such tests on the widest possible scale. The internist knows that he can prevent many strokes and premature heart attacks by encouraging his patients to have regular blood-pressure checkups, and it is his role to practice this type of preventive medicine. The pulmonologist is already assaulting lung cancer by promoting the curtailment of smoking. He has been indirectly responsible for the public-health warning that now appears on cigarette packages.

Because of the nature of his training, the psychiatrist feels most comfortable diagnosing and treating mental illness. But he has something more to offer: insight into some of

How psychiatry can help

the causes and effects of human behavior that affect government policy and the conduct of governing politicians. More than anyone else, the psychiatrist is able to infer deep and significant meanings from the speeches and actions of our politicians. He can offer an additional check and balance not provided in our Constitution.

The Nazis, unfortunately, realized this early, and were fearful of how the psychoanalytic movement of Sigmund Freud might serve as an obstacle to their nationalized psychosis. They guarded against this by their use of Carl Jung, one of Freud's best-known disciples. Jung's work became grist for the Nazi reinterpretation of psychoanalysis. This helped to protect the leadership of the Third Reich by diverting attention from insights into their own collective psychosis.

Can it happen here? Most Americans think that such a nightmare is not possible in our country. The fact that a book such as mine can be published and distributed certainly supports such optimism.

Perhaps, thanks to the Bill of Rights, our Constitution has anticipated the impossible after all—Spiro Agnew's most ardent wishes notwithstanding.

2

Steve Cleansman:
Prototype Portrait
of a
Lawyer / Politician

One of the greatest problems encountered in writing a book of this kind is making it comprehensible to the lay person. With the liberal use of psychiatric terminology, writing it would be easier; certainly it would be easier than making myself understood. As a psychiatrist approaching a psychiatric puzzle I am most comfortable (and certainly more agile) when I think in technical terms.

It is because I feel so strongly that the interested lay person has a right to understand some of the unusual, even frightening, phenomena surrounding Richard Nixon and his administration that I present this ostensibly fictional chapter. I am not concerned with the

The public's right to understand

Presidency or The President (as Nixon chooses to refer to himself); that falls more within the realm of the historian. Rather, it is Richard Nixon himself that I attempt to study here.

Who is Steve Cleansman? He is a very complicated product of my own imagination. By creating a fictional case history I can explain a series of very complicated interrelating psychological phenomena (psychodynamics) which can occur in the evolution of a lawyer/politician. The making of a lawyer/politician does not begin in law school; it begins shortly after birth. Understanding Steve Cleansman will facilitate understanding Richard Nixon, some of his closest aides, and Watergate and other recent events.

No "Freudian" speculations

I intend for the reader to understand some abstract psychiatric principles with a minimum of technical language. Once the principles of this next chapter have been ingested, they can be digested and synthesized in the course of the discussion in later chapters. A thorough knowledge of psychiatry should not have to be a prerequisite for significant insights into what has become a series of unprecedented national disasters.

I am not trying to produce more fuel for heated cocktail-party political gossip by adding

ill-defined psychopolitical speculations pep-
pered with "Freudian" nomenclature. That
would be irresponsible. I have read psychohistorical accounts of political figures in which
there is an obsession with such concepts as
"Oedipus Complexes" and "death instincts."
With the exception of a psychiatrist writing
about his own patient, the liberal use of these
concepts leads to a meaningless disaster.

I am referring to the classic analytic interpretations, which to be valid require the
most exacting knowledge about a person's
childhood development. To obtain such
knowledge the observer must interpret dreams
and listen to numerous hours of a patient's as-
sociative thinking; that is, the analyst must
allow the patient to talk about whatever comes
into his mind in an ongoing, uninhibited
fashion.

Because to date no author has had such a
direct opportunity with Nixon, studies such as
Mazlish's "psychohistory," which depends
upon classic theory, can have only very limited
application. Conversely, because *my* theoretical framework does not depend upon such
impossible-to-obtain material (e.g., Nixon's
dreams), it assumes considerably greater
plausibility.

**The trouble
with
"psychohistory"**

How could so many lawyers be involved?

I am introducing Steve Cleansman for yet other reasons. First of all, intimate useful background history on Richard Nixon and Co. is and probably always will be so scant as to make psychohistorical formulations almost useless. Second, I intend to answer directly the question posed by millions (among them former White House Counsel John Dean): "How could so many people in the law profession become so heavily involved in such a panorama of illegalities?"

A great deal can be learned from Steve Cleansman, and I have therefore spared few details of his background. He will serve as the stand-in for the real "stuntmen" to be studied later. So we will hear about Steve frequently throughout the remainder of this book.

While it is probably unnecessary, a word of caution may be appropriate. Steve Cleansman is not intended to be representative of everyone in the law profession or in politics. I surmise that his type accounts for a minority of lawyer/politicians.

3

Steve Cleansman:

From Uterus to Utopia

We begin our examination in Marysville, Kansas, in the summer of 1938, where and when the prototypical Steve Calvin Cleansman was born. The oldest of four children, Steve was the product of a middle-class family, and he arrived during a period of economic and psychological depression.

His father was a local butcher, who moonlighted weekends as a security guard in a dance hall that attracted college students. Steve's mother stayed at home most of the time but she was very active in the Marysville Methodist Church. Steve's younger brother, Tom, was well-known as the town delinquent; his reputation was based mainly upon his pug-

Meet the family

25

nacity, reckless driving, and wanton vandalism. Steve's younger sister Barbara married just after her high-school graduation and lives with her husband and two children on a farm just across the border in Nebraska. His youngest sister, now twenty-four, was a victim of a birth injury and is moderately mentally retarded; she continues to reside with her elderly parents in Marysville.

Growing up in the small Kansas town was not easy for the Cleansman children. Father was an inconsistent family provider, and he was chronically unhappy. A passive individual, he seldom had much to say about anything. His pessimistic and cynical attitude was infectious and much of the time shared by most of the family. Like his income, his personality was at times inconsistent with itself.

Father's tragedy
Perhaps Father's greatest tragedy was the apparent delight he derived in being hypercritical and belligerent when he drank. Though his drinking was not constant or even frequent, the resulting behavior left lasting impressions on the entire family.

Beneath his passive, tortoiselike exterior was a bitter, unhappy, hostile monster who, frightened of his own anger, could expose himself only with the aid of alcohol. But even during his sober moments one could see evidence of this angry self. At the butcher shop, wielding the meat cleaver, he often took on the appearance of a savage animal ravaging the kill. Butchering was more than a job for this man; it was a substitution as well as a sublimation for his intense hatred of himself and others.

He likewise derived perverse pleasure from his moonlighting job as a security guard. He was most effective in getting rid of drunken, unruly college students, who had "too much learnin' and not enough disciplinin'." The policemanlike uniform he wore even added some dignity to his pear-shaped abdomen. Following a busy weekend at the dance hall he would boast to the family how he "taught those kids something they ain't going to learn in college."

The pleasures of moonlighting

As the figurehead in the matriarchal household, Mr. Cleansman had an effect on everyone, but Steve seemed to suffer most. Perhaps this was because the groundwork was laid by Mrs. Cleansman. She was only seventeen when she married Steve's father and gave birth to Steve six months later. Inexperienced as a wife and mother, she got very little support from Mr. Cleansman. Her tremendous insecurity about caring for an infant led to worries about doing a poor job.

Mother hovered

In an attempt to compensate for unsureness, she hovered over baby Steve almost constantly. She never tolerated his crying in the night. She would change his diapers fifteen to twenty times daily in an effort to avoid prolonged wetness and consequent rashes. (Ironically, she would clean him so thoroughly and vigorously that he developed a rash from the hygiene ritual.) As he became a toddler, Mother continued to hover and overprotect her first-born, and would insist that he never play out of her view. She was intolerant of her son having any playmates, because he might then come into contact with a virus.

Though Steve was basically a healthy child, he was certainly not robust, and despite Mother's efforts to control his health, problems occurred. At the age of three Steve was a frail, clinging, helpless little boy suffering from intermittent abdominal symptoms. Usually, when he was under some kind of emotional stress he would develop cramping pain in the lower abdomen, sometimes accompanied by diarrhea. The condition was generally diagnosed by the family doctor as either a virus or mild food poisoning.

From a very early age Steve sensed his mother's obvious feelings of inadequacy and insecurity, which were conveyed in her actions. (Children probably are aware of a mother's degree of confidence from the first days of life. They sense this from the mother's tone of voice and degree of muscle tone. The latter provides some index of the amount of tension one is feeling.) More and more, Steve himself began to feel insecure, and his behavior showed it. The young boy would cling to his mother almost constantly and would become upset with her short absences while she attended church meetings. Father would respond to Steve's behavior by mocking him, jeering at him, and calling him "a little sissy."

The beginnings of insecurity

As could be expected, this served to exacerbate the boy's feeling of inadequacy and undermine his sense of masculinity. By the age of four he viewed his world as a frightening, threatening place of inevitable doom. More and more, Steve became sensitive to his father's criticism and began to resent the man for this. At the same time he was building up a resentment for his mother, because he sensed his own exaggerated dependence upon her. While these feelings were strong, Steve was unable to express them for fear of the consequences. Whenever the relationship with his parents became particularly strained, his gastrointestinal problem came to the surface, in lieu of his anger.

Toilet training as a power struggle

Another problem related to Steve's toilet habits. Despite his age, he remained only partially toilet trained. This provided a further source of crisis for Mrs. Cleansman, especially because she was keenly aware that Steve had to start school within a year. On the other hand, for Steve the conflict over toilet training provided a source of leverage. He could use it to control his mother, or at least avenge himself. Certainly, nobody but Steve could affect any control over his own performance at the toilet —and this was practically the only aspect of his life that could be almost totally regulated by him.

Especially important was the fact that mother was quite concerned over Steve's performance on the stool. Steve, of course, was aware of this fact. And so the toilet became the focal point of an important power struggle between Steve and his mother. At times her demands that he produce were met by resistance in the form of refusal. Overwhelmed by his mother's hovering and his father's ridicule, Steve could also, through judicious use of his bowels, retaliate in a limited way. By alternately accommodating and resisting parental demands, Steve acquired impressive expertise at manipulating his mother and father.

But toilet problems did not trigger the major crisis when Steve started school. Reluctant to leave his clinging mother, the boy was eventually forced by Father to start kindergarten. Separation from Mother left Steve with overwhelming feelings of helplessness—and intractable abdominal pain. Since the usual symptomatic treatment failed to bring about a remission, an appendectomy was performed at Marysville Memorial Hospital. The appendix appeared normal to the examining pathologist, who ruled out acute appendicitis, but Steve nevertheless quickly recovered from his pain, and from surgery as well. In two weeks he was back at school and apparently functioning well.

The pain of first separation

At first Steve despised school, because he felt homesick. Later he began to realize that he was brighter than many of his classmates. As he proceeded into the first grade of the moderately large country school, he found reading and arithmetic to be simple and achieved perfect grades in almost everything.

Only perfection counts

As he excelled in his school work his self-confidence began to increase slightly. But when he proudly brought home an *almost* perfect report card, his father zeroed in on an imperfect grade with ridicule and disgust. His self-righteous mother amplified this inappropriate criticism by telling the boy: "One should always work to the best of one's ability."

Such ludicrous clichés were more than a motto for the saintly Mrs. Cleansman: They aere her simplistic philosophy of life. Heavily steeped in religious fundamentalism, she tended to think in superlatives.

Trying harder and harder

Driven by his transient feelings of security and accomplishment, as well as by parental criticism, Steve tried even harder at school. He was now striving incessantly for perfection in school and in every other area of his life. His quest for perfection was propelled primarily by three forces:

1. His school accomplishments served momentarily to slacken deep-seated feelings of uncertainty.
2. His father's resentment and criticism always destroyed any temporary illusion of

infallibility or perfection; this motivated Steve to further perfectionistic efforts.

3. Mother's idealistic obsession with the church made her appear a paragon; Steve felt it was his duty to live up to this example.

The Marysville Methodist Church was a fundamentalist fire-and-brimstone organization and demanded much from its parishioners. Beginning with the Ten Commandments, the institution insisted upon paragonlike behavior. Not to be outdone by any other church, its own numerous and negative extra-biblical commandments added up to a veritable Chinese menu of taboos. Out of preternatural respect for Marysville Methodist, Mother preached to her children an almanac of virtues by which to live. The "Thou shalt nots" covered everything from smoking and drinking to masturbation and unsanctified sexuality.

With the exception of Steve and his unfortunate sister, the family rejected Mother's de facto role as preacher. For Steve, the carefully outlined prescription of church mores fit well into his ongoing quest for quintessence.

Methodism also served to channel (in a most subtle but vicious way) his considerable hatred

More than ten commandments

The first feelings of superiority

for his father. Because the church taught that it was wrong to hate, Steve labeled his father a sinner who would, hopefully (and, of course, rightfully), go to hell. With religious zeal he could castigate the man for his despicable drinking and other sinful activities. This not only played into Steve's gravitation toward perfection, but gave rise to feelings of superiority. By looking down on his father, through the condescending eyes of the church, Steve could further elevate his own self-esteem at Daddy's expense.

A grandiose, self-righteous flavor gradually blended into the young man's personality. By the age of ten he was strongly identifying himself with his mother and acquiescing to the demands of the church. His own artificially inflated image of himself turned him into an auxiliary authority around the house. Indeed, Steve demanded—and received—undue amounts of respect and prestige from the entire rest of the family.

The uneasiness never stopped

Beneath the superhuman exterior, however, lifelong feelings of unsureness were Steve's constant companions. Feelings of uneasiness about himself were ever present, never really remitting. With a backdrop of these anxious remnants of early infancy and childhood, Steve was perpetually driven by a vague anticipation of impending doom. Sometimes he experienced this in the form of guilt feelings about his afflicted sister. While praying in church he asked God why, for example, he was allowed to be normal and his sister retarded. Deep down, the boy's opinion of himself was really not very good: He felt that someone as lowly as himself was entitled to very little in life. He even felt that in some vague way he might somehow have been responsible for his sister's misfortune.

Early signs of omnipotence

What on the surface appeared to be empathy for the retarded sister was really early evidence of Steve's omnipotent posture. He felt responsible for her condition as well as other phenomena; as a result, he began to feel powerful at times. At other times he felt fearful and guilty about his imagined potency. This dichotomy was a prelude to other inconsistent, ambivalent feelings.

An emerging problem concerned decision making. This problem, like many others, related back to Steve's strivings toward perfection in an attempt to deny the phenomenal uncertainties about himself. In trying to make a decision of any kind, he thought in terms of extremes: Everything was either black or white; there were no shades of gray. Any compromising decision was tantamount to total unfulfillment. There could be no room for such hedging or fence sitting. After all, if a person is to be consummate, he must be totally decisive in a superlative sense. Every decision, therefore, must have either an absolutely positive answer or an absolutely negative answer. Steve could not afford to risk arriving at a wrong answer; this would invalidate his comforting feelings of omniscience.

Decisions paralyzed him

Consequently, when confronted with decisions, he was paralyzed. In order not to risk rupturing his infallibility, he put off the task as long as possible. He vacillated during this period and seemed to weigh all the possibilities forever. Finally, when necessity forced him to act, he would do so impulsively, in a moment of panic. As previously mentioned, Mrs. Cleansman tended to think in superlatives, and this understandably facilitated her son's difficulties: His decisions not only had to be right—they had to be super-right.

Steve proceeded through grade school and junior high, accumulating numerous friends, but none ever got to know him very intimately. In order to maintain the comforting illusion of omniscience and omnipotence it was necessary for our young prototype to maintain full control over all aspects of life. In the context of friendships, this need dictated that Steve not get emotionally close to anyone. On the other hand, he took pride in becoming a confidant for others. This meshed well into the young boy's need to control, for as his friends confided in him, they were in effect offering themselves to Steve for a certain amount of emotional subjugation.

This very busy one-way thoroughfare paved the way for Steve to become the undisputed leader in school and church peer-group activities. He amassed some insight into everybody; they, on the other hand, knew little about his inner life, because he never allowed them to find out about his real feelings. The structure of Steve's interrelationships resembled a submarine. Lurking beneath the water surface and peering into the submarine's periscope, the captain is able to enjoy a 360-degree view of the world. His safety is guaranteed by his anonymity. This puts him at an advantage over others. Potentially, it places him in a position of power.

The road to leadership

Young Steve's submarine was his fluid personality: He displayed a façade of friendliness and warmth which, while attracting people, also acted as a camouflage for his real thoughts and feelings. The inadvertent release of candor would be equivalent to allowing the submarine to surface, be exposed, and be subject to devastation at any time. Like a submarine, the boy was able to maneuver around his friends while never showing himself without his inhibitions.

Treating people as objects

This personality stance permitted Steve to manipulate and take advantage of people as though they were objects. And thanks to all these carefully executed maneuvers, the boy's sense of grandiosity gained further altitude. Inevitably (and not unexpectedly) he was elected president of the church choir and vice-president of his eighth-grade class. These responsibilities involved attendance at a variety of meetings with the clergy, teachers, and students where the fluidity of Steve's demeanor provided an impressive element of diplomacy that served him well in dealing with these people.

Working on school and church projects required little in the way of creative activity, but rather an inordinate amount of busywork. Being highly organized and perfectionistic, Steve seemed to function smoothly and eventually (as a high school junior) was elected treasurer of the student council. The job fit him like a contour chair. It required compulsive, meticulous, orderly attention to charting the debits and credits of the student treasury, and again the "submarine effect" came into play: Steve had a full accounting of who had paid and, even more important, who owed. Again, then, he was given access to information (intelligence) in a one-way fashion. After all, the class dues had an aura of confidentiality about them, and only Steve should rightly know such (to him) vital information.

The contour of the job conformed to yet another aspect of his mental anatomy. As previously shown, Steve was obsessed with such issues as right versus wrong, good versus bad, and moral versus immoral. To him, shades of gray could not exist, and so it was paramount always to be right, good, and moral. This led to a policemanlike attitude toward people; it was mandatory that people always live up to our paragon's expectations—which were impossible to attain in the first place. Collecting dues became a one-man crusade for Steve. It was not so much a matter of balancing the minuscule student budget. The real issue was altruism, to see that everyone acquiesced to the Cleansman standard of excellence.

Everything was black or white

Emotional necessity also dictated that Steve be a *perfect* treasurer; his reputation was on the line (and, likewise, his emotional integrity was at stake). He could not be a *fairly* good treasurer, because again he demanded all-or-nothing of himself. In his view there could be only excellent or terrible treasurers, and even one unpaid member would equal total failure. Not surprisingly, this treasurer set a school record: All 358 students in the school paid dues.

Perfection made him president

Steve spent inordinate amounts of time and effort to make the 100-percent collection a reality. And soon his success became an effective campaign issue in his successful bid for the student council presidency.

While the Cleansmans were pleased over their son's accomplishment, they were bemused by his paradoxical reaction to his latest and so far greatest achievement. A sullen, somewhat anxious victor, Steve was unhappy over what he felt to be an undeserved reward. His running for president had been an attempt to overcome insecurities by proving himself. Ironically, the new responsibilities and duties that were required of him served to reawaken self-uncertainties. Steve was frightened of his own heightened power and felt inadequate to handle the job.

In the treasury job the work plan was well charted. While its execution demanded tremendous effort, it asked little in the way of innovation. Collecting and computing dues did not require the making of any decisions and therefore presented no emotional risks.

The new position demanded both creativity and decisiveness, and for Steve this proved overwhelming. Once more, because of underlying feelings of doubt, the nervous boy found himself immobilized by ambivalence. As he saw his new role, effecting a decision—even the most trivial kind—offered the fifty-fifty opportunity of effecting a mistake. Every act of decision equaled a potential blunder, which, in turn, threatened his need for total control and ultimately chipped away at the caricature of his own grandiosity. Stripped of this inflated blanket of security, Steve would be left exposed, and others might see him as the humiliated mass of anxiety and uncertainty that he really was. Temporary infallibility could be maintained only if a decision could be delayed.

The doubts were overwhelming

When presented with a challenging (any) decision in a student council meeting, Steve therefore chose to "take the matter under advisement so as to consider all angles of the problem before choosing to act." This ploy caused him to become admired as a veritable King Solomon who acted wisely after using a methodical, analytic, problem-solving approach.

Making indecision look like wisdom

In actuality, nothing could have been further misperceived: While it appeared that Steve was meticulously analyzing, he was really hopelessly vacillating in order to avoid the challenge of having to stick his neck out. As the deadline for decisiveness approached, Steve would choose impulsively. And so, although he was ambivalent, insecure, and impulsive in his grasp of a problem, Steve maintained the illusion of a wise, calculating judge. The resulting misguided admiration of his underlings furthered his feelings of omniscience.

But this did not solve the decision making dilemma itself. His procrastination and impulsivity led occasionally to misguided choices. It is interesting to see how Steve worked around his nemesis: impulsivity.

Curbing his impulsivity

Steve's ability to manipulate (if not exploit) people was a keenly developed talent that made him a successful council president. But he had to overcome one major personal difficulty: In a way, he was too unsure of himself to take full control of a situation and thereby risk blame or responsibility for failure. On the other hand, he also needed to maintain control of his position—and thereby perpetuate his delusion of infallibility. We now discover that our young politician was bright and clever despite his inability to innovate. The problem he faced can be schematized as follows: °

1. I need to be in full control of a situation in order to preserve my infallibility.
2. If, however, I am in full control of a situation, I am also responsible for the outcome of that situation.

Cleansman could not synthesize this (or any other) dichotomy with any degree of confidence. He chose instead to manipulate around the matter by distributing all decision making to fellow officers and committeemen.

Now he could take credit for their successes. In the event of failure the blame, of course, was placed on the subordinate's inability to carry out Steve's policy. Steve was thus insured

Insurance against failure

°This not-so-hypothetical dichotomy should have a familiar ring to the high-echelon Watergate principals.

against the risk of failure, and his insatiable appetite for being in the right could now be fed. He had his cake and could eat it too.

This further fit into his scheme of grandiosity, for it is obvious that Steve created a situation in which he was given *special privilege*.

To clarify this important concept: Steve could take credit for the successes of his appointed underlings, but in a reverse situation (if, for example, the committee performed poorly), Steve could blame failure on the committee. So by *special privilege* I mean that Steve created for himself an immunity from having to take blame but he could enjoy and feel indirectly responsible for successes. He could anticipate praise for achievements and exemption from any fiascos.

Success led to depression The anxieties of becoming council president led to feelings of depression; Steve had achieved success, but that same achievement presented grand opportunities for failure. (Any opportunity to prove offers an equal opportunity to disprove.)

While Steve had "fully insured" himself against failure in one situation, his inflexibility left him unprepared for the new situation. Steve went from a situation of total control (student council treasurer) to one of poor control (student council president). For many people each new challenge at first is seen as a crisis. This results in feelings of uneasiness —anxiety, depression—that are not relieved until the situation is brought under control. As president Steve was eventually able to maneuver around his decision-making responsibilities; once he did this, his superficial sense of confidence returned. Our aspiring politician warded off his depression by shifting into a flurry of activity, mostly in the form of maneuvering himself away from areas of decision and instead manipulating cohorts into those dangerous areas.

Rather than participate in such decision making, he appointed committees to handle most matters. Throughout his successful year as student council president he manipulated and exploited associates, avoided making suggestions of his own, and perpetuated the illusion of one who was so unconcerned about power that he humbly allowed others to share responsibilities.

Manipulation through committees

As Steve proceeded into college, these patterns not only recycled but metamorphosed. Again he did fairly well academically and was successful in campus politics, but, as always, he maintained very guarded relationships with people. He pledged a fraternity and became well-liked by everybody while he continued to maintain a safe distance. A charming diplomat, Steve came to know everyone well and therefore knew what they liked to hear. He was liberal with liberals, rebellious with rebels, and independent with the apathetic. By avoiding overt disagreements he provided further insurance against criticism. While it was difficult to get involved with Steve, it was even more difficult to hate him. His obsequious behavior led to another rapid political triumph: While only a junior he was elected president of the fraternity.

No sense of humor

Certain other elements of his personality were now coming more openly into play. Three days after his election, and without warning, he was thrown, fully clothed, into the shower by his fraternity brothers. Though the incident was supposed to be only a silly initiation rite, Steve reacted to the joke by getting up out of the shower and impulsively tackling one of his initiators. He summarily threw the startled victim into the shower and bloodied the young man's face until the others terminated the regrettable episode. The event domonstrated that Steve did not like surprises and seemed to lack a sense of humor.

In fact, Steve had never in his life demon-strated that he possessed any wit or humor. He was too obsessed with the maintenance of con-trol to allow such traits to develop. A sense of humor demands a certain amount of emotional laxity, a dash of candor, a bit of looseness. An overly serious, guarded, rigid personality such as Steve's cannot tolerate even the transient loosening of the reins that real humor requires.

In the same way and for the same reasons, Steve could not tolerate surprises, especially not the kind that results in self-humiliation. Much of his behavior and energy were chan-neled into making sure that his future would be *safe*. This reexplains in part the incessant need to be completely organized, ready for anything. It was yet another way to avoid the risk of failure, a new variation of an old, driving theme.

No tolerance for surprises

Since, by definition, one cannot prepare specifically for a surprise, this element was highly threatening to Steve. It did not fit well into his plan for life. Because Steve's emotional interplays with people were contrived and preplanned, his fraternity's practical joke was a shattering experience. The situation descended upon him without warning, so his reaction could not be prepared. This explains the inappropriate, even violent reaction, in the form of impulsive retaliation.

Losing control is worst of all

For several days following the incident Steve was afraid to face his fraternity brothers, so he returned home, seeking the security of his mother. During the weekend visit his mood was one of grief. He had done the thing that he feared most: Though only momentarily, Steve had *lost control* of himself, exposed some of his real feelings, allowed some candor to slip out. The submarine had suddenly surfaced without the prelude of the usual alarm warning signal.

The incident also brought to light a curious contradiction. Steve always enjoyed carrying out a practical joke, especially if the joke was executed by a team. This penchant represents another part of the submarine analogy. As the jok*er* one is placed in a relative position of power over the jok*ee*. And by participating with others in arranging a joke, there is built-in protection against individual retaliation on the part of the jokee. And with Steve there existed a very real fear of retaliation, based on his own conscious awareness of how he might react if he were to be the jokee.

When the joke is on the other foot

There is also the delight in seeing someone else (the jokee in this case) humiliated and/or out of control. After all, if one is the humilia*tor*, one cannot be the humiliat*ee*. Steve's enjoyment in participating in a practical joke therefore did not arise from a sense of humor; rather, it demonstrated a sadistic feeling which, when gratified, led to feelings of self-security.

As he finished undergraduate studies, Steve began to sense that he might be cut out for the law profession. This was to be one of the greatest insights of his life.

With his fluid personality, he was soon on the good side of most of his law professors, but it was in law school that he ran into another crisis. High school and college had been relatively easy for our clever prototype, but law school presented him with a unique and overwhelming challenge. We have already become all too aware of Steve's pursuit of perfection. And he had always been concerned with a knowledge of all details in all situations. (Familiarity breeds security.) So if, theoretically, Steve could know everything about every subject, he could then be prepared for the unknown. There would then be no unknown, because omniscience makes the unknown known.

In his law studies our aspiring attorney was therefore acutely afraid to leave out anything. If an omission were to occur, something important might be overlooked. In undergraduate

Preparation through overkill

school this indiscriminate, sweeping approach was possible to some extent, but not in law school. As Steve attempted to familiarize himself with the total contents of the school's law library, he consciously realized the impossibility of his efforts. But unconsciously he nevertheless was driven to accomplish the superhuman, the perfect, the unattainable.

In attacking law briefs he marshaled the technique of overkill. He spent thirty hours on a weekend over-researching a minor case that could have been presented competently in a busy afternoon. In a quest to consume the world's knowledge of law, Steve found himself expending prodigious amounts of energy and accomplishing little. It was not so much that Steve couldn't see the forest for the trees. Rather, he was trying to examine all the trees with a microscope. He soon found that his inability to distinguish trivia from important facts was hurting his performance, and he gravitated to the lower middle third of his class—a position he could hardly reconcile with his feelings of grandiosity.

Exempt from the rules   You will recall that Steve, in his self-deluded grandiosity, felt a certain exemption from the general rules of society. He first demonstrated this while high school Student Council president and later in his ability to be a joker but not a jokee. (Actually, the first germ of this trait was demonstrated much earlier in Steve's one-way "submarine relationships.") Under the influence of self-made grandiosity, Steve saw himself as enjoying special privileges. Exempt from the usual rules of society, he marched to his own drumming.

But his grandiosity provided him with a solution to his mediocre performance in law school: He began to cheat. His cheating, though, had a unique quality about it: Unlike many cheaters, he suffered little, if any, uneasiness or guilt. Again, grandiosity provides the explanation. For Steve cheating was not wrong (although he felt it would be for his classmates); it was a special privilege, something from which he was even able to derive a feeling of pride.

Another quality that made Steve's cheating unique was that he had no fear of being caught (as most cheaters would). In the milieu of his own omnipotence he was deluded into thinking that he was immune from being discovered. Just as he was exempt from the usual ethics that forbid cheating, he was immune to the consequences.

No fear of being caught

The law school honor system facilitated

Steve's unethical endeavors, and, ironically, he became determined to turn in anyone whom he might detect cheating. Having developed a very "close" relationship with a particular professor, he simultaneously opened a safe line of intelligence communication. He used this privileged relationship to turn in two class-mates whom he once suspected of cheating. Because of his confidential relationship with Professor Donewright, Steve could snitch on his classmates without fear of retaliation; in effect, he became the de facto class policeman without risking the popularity he enjoyed. Infrequently Steve continued to expose the cheaters, who, in all cases, had higher academic standing than himself.

A poignant performance   Steve's carefully contrived utopia disintegrated midway through his third year at the law school: He was turned in by a classmate for submitting a brief that had been prepared by another classmate for a small fee. Ironically, Steve would never have been caught had he not bragged to someone about "pulling it off." (Maybe this is really not so ironic after all, when we recall that Steve never really considered cheating a risk.)

Steve was called before the dean and assistant dean of the Law College, and they threatened to expel him. The fluidity of Steve's personality, in conjunction with his ability to manipulate and maneuver, saved the day. While choking on his own tears, our young lawyer laid out his whole "life story." It was a combination of Hollywood and Horatio Alger: the poignant prologue of a boy from Marysville who represented his parents' only hope for vicarious success. Driven by a desire to make his parents proud, he had now, "for the first time ever," given in to his "worse judgment" and committed an "overzealous but immoral act."

(This scenario may at first glance appear to be an inconsistency, for Steve seems to be displaying feelings. Actually, it is a contrivance; with calculated humility Steve is still manipulating, albeit in a passive manner.)

The scene in the dean's office was a study in contrived self-pity, and the pinnacle of manipulations. When Steve Cleansman was finished with his controlled outpouring, the dean and assistant dean felt guilty for having insisted on the meeting in the first place.

Upon graduation, our lawyer joined the ranks of a reasonably prestigious law firm and manipulated his way into politics. Liberal use of his established exploitative and manipulative

More and more grandiosity

mechanisms continued to come naturally to him. As he ascended the political ladder, his grandiose feelings heightened geometrically. He made and used numerous "friends" and again developed the reputation of a calculating, methodical paragon of coolness; his "decisions" were looked upon as refined logical deductions.

In a way reminiscent of the days when he was student council treasurer and undercover policeman of his law class, his primary campaign issue was, not surprisingly, "law and order." Consistent with his general modus operandi, he granted and received numerous special favors from people. All of his maneuvers were carried out with a feeling of pride and little concern over exposure.

The rest is history.

The purpose of this case history

The preceding case history is not meant to be a mirror image or even an approximate replica of Richard Nixon's psychology, or of anyone else's in particular. In fact, I wrote this chapter prior to my research into Nixon's early life. But I was gratified by certain coincidences that struck me as I briefed myself on Nixon's youth.

These coincidences further convinced me that I was heading in the right direction.

For example, after finishing the Cleansman case history I discovered that Richard Nixon in law school, fearing the competition of many Phi Beta Kappas, compulsively out-studied many of his classmates in a quantitative compensatory effort because he feared failure and loss of a scholarship.

More important, I would not want the reader to lose sight of the real purpose of this chapter. It is to demonstrate the dynamics of certain personality mechanisms. The anecdotal case history format makes it unnecessary to use confusing jargon. And so Steve Cleansman is not a prototype of Nixon, Haldeman, et al.; he is a blackboard on which I have sketched some of the personality mechanisms utilized by Nixon and most of my other subjects.

Steve Cleansman is not a prototype of any person; he is a prototype of the defense mechanisms used by many persons. It is a device to make our study of Nixon and his associates somewhat easier.

4

The Nixon Profile

The psychiatric examination of any patient presents problems for the examiner even when there is full cooperation—for example, a cooperative but overzealous patient may respond in a way calculated to please his examiner.

This problem is minuscule compared to a situation that offers no interplay at all, and this is of course the case when profiling in absentia. For these and other reasons, the psychiatric examination of Richard Milhous Nixon presents something of an ultimate challenge. Although he has been an internationally known figure for over two decades, the personal information known about him is surprisingly thin.

The profiler's big problem

In analyzing his early life I have depended heavily on material furnished by his biographers. More can be learned about the product of that early life by observing the man through his own writings. It is gratifying to discover that my initial impressions and observations of Nixon (especially over television in the last four years) mesh well into the psychological matrix of his childhood and maturity. Cause-and-effect relationships do emerge.

Looking for causes, not effects

Earl Mazo's *Nixon—A Political Portrait* and Ralph De Toledano's *One Man Alone* contain considerable information detailing Nixon's climb from Yorba Linda, California (his birthplace), to the Presidency. Yet these and other publications, while informative, deal more with the effects of Richard Nixon than his causes. Only through analysis of this raw material can we move closer to our subject.

Occasionally Nixon biographers attempt to describe a humorous or poignant, personally revealing situation, in an effort to allow readers to feel some degree of closeness to their subject. Unfortunately, these episodes tend to fall short of promoting the intended flavor of candor. The apparent lack of candor is not a reflection on Nixon's biographers—it is an inevitable extension of their subject matter. Evans and Novak *(Nixon in the White House)* speak of the President's "passion for privacy" and describe Nixon as "the most inaccessible President since Herbert Hoover."

In delineating the psychology of Nixon, I will show how he can remain *psychologically* covert or private even when he is appearing in public—except on very rare, extremely stressful occasions. Through Nixon's command over emotion and thought, he usually allows the public to see only what he feels he can afford to let it see.

Staying psychologic-ally covert

When he is talking about himself Nixon is particularly feeble in his apparent efforts to allow the reader a closer look. His famous "Checkers" speech is a classic example. During the 1952 campaign Nixon, the Vice-Presidential candidate, was accused of using a special $18,000 campaign fund maintained by a group of California fat cats. He salvaged his tenuous position as a candidate through the nationally televised "Checkers" rebuttal. In *Six Crises*, Nixon's own, limited, and highly selective autobiography, we are given his account of the famous speech. With an air of humility he sarcastically spoke of the personal campaign contributions he had indeed accepted. Among them was a dog "contributed" by a man from Texas who had heard Pat Nixon say in an aside on a radio broadcast that her daughters would love to have one. Nixon quotes a portion of the speech:

The psychological significance of Checkers

"It was a little cocker spaniel dog in a crate that he had sent all the way from Texas—black and white, spotted, and our little girl Tricia, the six-year-old, named it Checkers. And you know, the kids, like all kids, loved the dog, and I just want to say this, right now, that regardless of what they say about it, we are going to keep it."

A casual reading of this passage could bring a tear to the reader's eye, but my psychiatric appraisal of this most meaningful speech later in these pages will reveal it to be anything but a touching glimpse of what many still search for more than twenty years afterward: the "real Nixon."

Theoretically, my psychiatric analysis of Nixon falls (admittedly) short of the real thing; I have never met my subject. So my approach is flawed in that respect. But the direct approach will not and probably cannot occur, and I do not in any way advocate it. In fact, I will state my professional judgment that Richard Nixon probably is not in need of psychiatric treatment, as of this writing.

Though it has been suggested by Mazlish *(In Search of Nixon)* that Nixon may (according to Drew Pearson) have undergone four and one-half years of psychotherapy, I think that any future contacts with a psychiatrist would be most unlikely. Mazlish, drawing from Joe McGinniss *(The Selling of the President 1968)*, quotes a Nixon aide as describing Nixon's hatred for psychiatrists and how they make him nervous.

Nixon hates psychiatrists

Nixon's early suspicions of the psychiatric profession are documented as far back as 1933. With this as a backdrop, the burglarizing of Dr. Lewis Fielding's office (he was Ellsberg's psychiatrist) not only seems less surprising but takes on a second meaning. Nixon's anxiety around psychiatrists is in itself revealing, and I will explain it at a more appropriate juncture.

Even if Nixon were to consult a psychiatrist, and if that psychiatrist's records were obtainable, it is likely that not much additional insight would be gained into the man. The pieces of the puzzle are already available, and one need not resort to a subpoena of records or to burglary to find them. I am confident that even in his one-to-one confidential relationships Nixon reveals little. One-to-one relationship with a doctor would be no different.

No need for more data

The fact that I have never met the man becomes, therefore, less of a disadvantage for me than it would be in another situation with a more open "patient." De Toledano sustains my contentions:

In his speeches, his writings, and his conversation Richard Nixon has said less about himself than any major public figure of the twentieth century. To this day those who probe into the kitchen middens of his life cannot say with certainty what his religion is or precisely where he stands on a hundred issues that his rhetoric has touched. Those like myself who have known him, who have seen him in crisis and triumph, can only approximate the nature and meaning of this introvert *who chose for himself the extrovert life of politics.* . . . Nixon has baffled armchair and professional psychologists. . . .

Through my own observations and research of the man, I feel that I have acquainted myself with the real Richard Nixon, directly, indirectly, and adequately. I would now like to introduce him to you, the reader.

To say that a psychiatric profile of Richard Nixon must be based on extensive knowledge of his early childhood is to say that the task cannot be done at all. On this point—the genesis of our subject—I most vigorously depart from other psychological and psychohistorical works that have been assembled on Nixon. These writings tend to postulate that Nixon's personality is a product of specific sibling rivalries, sibling guilt, certain unfulfilled subconscious wishes, and Oedipal complexities. While such jargon-heavy suggestions are historically interesting, and probably true in a vague, general sense, they are psychoanalytically naive.

The seeds of Nixon's insecurity

Not enough is known of Richard the child to set up such formulations with any degree of validity. My theories require knowledge only of the general flavor experienced by this child as he tasted life in this very early period. It is my intention to present insight merely into a young, insecure boy growing up in early twentieth-century California. For this I believe genuine documentation exists.

Nixon was born in 1913 and was to be the second of five boys. His birthplace was Yorba Linda, a small farming community near Los Angeles.

His father's luckless career

Francis (Frank) Nixon, the head of the

household, was a striving man whose efforts were never to be significantly or directly rewarded. Mazo documents this by describing the extraordinary variety of his vocations: carpenter, orange and lemon rancher, trolley-car operator, general-store proprietor, and service-station manager. The man's luck was no better than his career suggests. A year after Frank Nixon decided between two tracts of land for his gasoline station, oil was discovered on the rejected land parcel. De Toledano characterizes Frank Nixon as a political liberal who enjoyed the challenge of argument. Mazo describes Frank's infuriation over the Teapot Dome scandal, which involved the corrupted Harding administration and its mishandling of government oil reserves.

Two very strong women

Nixon's mother, Hannah Milhous Nixon, has been described as a loving mother with an iron will and a sense of ambition for her entire family. Her mother, in turn, was an impressive woman who, according to Mazo and others, provided a cohesive force which held the family together over the years.

Like Steve Cleansman, Nixon was born into a family subjected to considerable economic uncertainty. Not only was life without its warranties—just existing was a burden. As De Toledano tells us:

"Richard Nixon was formed by a home life in which work and struggle were always present ... children shared the daily burdens ... there was little time to play. Even when the economic pressures eased slightly, the Nixons continued to live as if poverty lurked beyond every payday."

In addition to the constantly undermining threat of economic insecurity, Frank Nixon promoted another kind of threat within young Richard. He was quite a violent man and was often to be feared, especially during the course of an argument. This provides another similarity to Steve Cleansman's history: Mr. Nixon, like Mr. Cleansman, was a personage to be feared by his sons. Young Richard, fearful of his father's wrath and authoritarianism, was unable to gain self-confidence because he could not argue with the man and occasionally win.

From the teachings of Alfred Adler, a noted Viennese student of Freud, we know how critically important such a situation becomes. Children are by their very nature inferior to adults (height, weight, strength, life experience, I.Q., etc.), and in the process of

Fear of father

maturing they must continually strive to prove to themselves that they are not always—and therefore will not be always—weak and inferior. Adler tells us that self-confidence results from mastering situations throughout childhood, and so does a consequent sense of security.

No challenges allowed

There is evidence that Frank Nixon was himself too insecure to have allowed any challenges from his endeavoring offspring. (Evidence of Frank's insecurities is abundant and will be detailed later.) In important ways, then, his children were deprived of the satisfaction that can be derived from mastering and dominating.

In the Nixon context we can assume that, if Frank had been a more moderate father, he could have allowed his sons the necessity of some free expression and interchange. The man would then have instilled a greater sense of security and self-reliance into his children. That this never happened is shown by De Toledano:

"Nixon never stood up in an argument to his father, often counseling his brothers never to challenge Frank Nixon in a debate."

I am confident from my research that young

Richard Nixon avoided challenging his father in general, not just in debate.

We also know, from the same source, that when Nixon's older brother Harold was stricken with tuberculosis, the burden of responsibility was shouldered by young Richard. A variety of sources confirm that for approximately two years—a very long time by a child's calendar—Mrs. Nixon left Richard and the family behind to seek a cure for the ailing boy in arid Arizona. Apparently during that same time period, Richard's younger brother Arthur died, relatively suddenly, from tuberculous meningitis. Following Harold's return to California with his mother, he died of the more chronic form of the disease that had long been afflicting him.

In this context Mazlish and others postulate tenuous theories of sibling rivalry followed by sibling guilt presumably suffered by young Richard on the death of his brothers. Reference is made to "Oedipal features," and it is suggested that Richard must have been jealous of Harold for taking his mother away to Arizona. The conclusion, predicated on this jealousy, is that Harold's death was a source of tremendous guilt for Richard. While Mazlish's presumption

Burden of responsibility

is intriguing and fits well into classic analytic theory, it is also an example of what an armchair psychologist can read into a situation shrouded with unknowns. The Freudian leaps may be justified. But perhaps they are not.

The impact of tragedy   Concrete inferences can, however, be drawn from this tragic cluster of events, which probably began when Nixon was about twelve. As I will confirm further, Richard was quite close to his mother. Certainly her two-year absence must have been experienced as a bitter loss, albeit temporary. Not only was the transient separation premature, but it further burdened the boy—now the oldest at home—with more responsibilities. At a time in his life when he would have derived security from the presence of his two parents, he was forced to function as a partial substitute for one of them. De Toledano reports: "Richard and the other sons took on Mrs. Nixon's household tasks, cooking and cleaning, and helping with the store."

It would be difficult to overestimate the impact on Nixon of experiencing the death of an older and a younger brother in quick succession. While surviving the hard times himself, he was forced to face the grim reality that death can indeed strike even at a young (and therefore usually secure) age.

Most children below the age of eight or so comfort themselves under a cloak of artificial security that makes them feel somewhat omnipotent. The five-year-old does not worry about such matters seriously; he even has some difficulty imagining what death is in actuality, or realizing that it is real. Most children are allowed to mature and grow out of this feeling of naive security gradually; young Richard Nixon was jolted out of it—not once but twice—and at the age of twelve, too, this can leave serious effects.

Living with death

Even more important were the physical traumata directly experienced by young Richard. At the age of three Nixon was nearly killed in a buggy accident. To this day he continues to bear a scar where the heavy wheel grazed his head. He also nearly died of pneumonia at the age of four.

Trauma and illness are frightening at any age; at the ages of three and four respectively, they take on considerably greater significance. It is during this period in a child's life (between the ages of two and five) that he becomes most aware of his body's integrity and vulnerability.

Long-range effects of illness

Injury in the form of accident, illness, or surgery, when occurring during this age period, may leave lasting emotional scars in the form of anxiety and insecurity.

As adults these children may continue to experience the manifestations of this anxiety over their physical integrity. Anyone who has raised a child can probably attest to the overconcern of their two- or three-year-old with respect to minor scrapes and bumps. The severe, life-threatening trauma and illness in Nixon's early childhood therefore has significant bearing on his psychiatric history.

How religiosity was transmitted

The study of Richard Nixon's early years also must not overlook the family's religious fundamentalism and how it was transmitted by Hannah and Frank to their children. Mr. Nixon, we are told by Mazo, was a "Bible pounding Methodist" who upon marriage traded in his faith (at least symbolically) for his wife's. A variety of biographical sources use this and other examples to describe the family in matriarchal terms.

While much of the difference between "Bible pounding Methodism" and Hannah Milhous's Quakerism is probably academic, we should not overlook the significant fact that the Quaker label (not the Methodist) has always been an integral part of Richard Nixon. While I make little general differentiation between Hannah and Frank Nixon's religious fundamentalism, I would not want to overlook an important and unique aspect of Quakerism: The Quakers place great stress on pacifism. (The effects of this stress on Nixon will be discussed.)

A highly religious matriarch, Hannah Nixon was a hardworking, almighty woman, whose dominance in the family was amplified by making the church a partner in family authority. From De Toledano:

Mother drove the family

"Frank Nixon could hold forth in the family store, but Hannah drove herself and her family. Her day would begin at the first morning light, and the boys rose with *her*. The family ate breakfast together, saying their prayers and reciting Bible verses."

And so, just as Frank Nixon reminds us of the elder Mr. Cleansman, Hannah Milhous, a powerful agent of the church, resembles Mrs. Cleansman.

Not only was Bible reading something to be ingested with breakfast but Mazo tells of excessive church attendance. On Sunday the family attended four times. This was in addition to the usual weekday meetings. An ultimate

To church four times a day

indicator of Hannah's degree of religiosity was her statement after the death of her fourth son, Arthur, aged seven. Again from Mazo:

" 'It is difficult at times to understand the ways of our Lord, but we know that there is a plan and the best happens for each individual.' "

Plan, plan, plan   The key word is "plan." To the religious fundamentalist, inordinate comfort arises from the belief that everything has been planned and everything must be planned. We need only to reexamine Steve Cleansman to see how this mechanism works psychologically. If something has been planned and one follows that plan to the letter, no decisions need to be made. No independent judgments must then be made and acted upon. Therefore (and most important), no risks need be feared.

Working under this philosophy, the lack of a preexisting plan requires that one protect oneself from the unknown by making a plan. As treasurer of student council, Steve delighted in the security of his planned job. Initially insecure with his new job as student council president, he reduced his insecurities with elaborate planning. In this same way, I see a significant seed of psychological insecurity germinating in young Richard Nixon. With the influence of his ambitious and highly organized mother and church, we know that young Nixon was immersed in a religious concentrate that provided him with a planned philosophy of life and prescribed stringent mores and enormous respect for authority. Mazo supports this by reporting: "Much of Richard Nixon's early life centered at the East Whittier Friends Meeting House—the Quaker church."

For many children such highly concentrated fundamental religious experiences foster a great deal of dependence and submissiveness by stifling independence of thought. Fundamentalist churches readily supply firm answers to many difficult life questions and thereby make independence of thought unnecessary in many instances.

Learning to be dependent

When one is offered all but a complete prescription for life, one needs only to take the pill, follow the plan, do what one is told. Unwavering respect for authority is the real hallmark of religious fundamentalism. When overdone, it leads to fearfulness. Some children rebel against such a pious atmosphere (e.g., Steve Cleansman's brother, Tom), others acquiesce. When it came to the issue of respect for authority and the consequent need for discipline, young Nixon was not a rebel but an assenter.

"Richard took his spankings without a whimper," Mazo informs us.

Going along with the system

Nixon has himself described his father as having had a temper; others, including Frank's own wife, have described him as punitive. In this respect Frank Nixon was not unique for his time and cultural-religious background. Of greater import is the fact that early in life Richard Nixon must have sought comfort in going along with the long and firmly established system (Mother/Church/Father), rather than rebelling or acting to become independent of it. Furthermore, we know that young Nixon, like his mother, was highly organized and a planner. Again from Mazo: "Nixon's brother Donald recalls that 'Dick always planned things out. He didn't do things accidentally. . . . He had more of Mother's traits than the rest of us.' "

Here we see another very important pattern reminiscent of Steve Cleansman: Young Nixon gravitated toward his mother while, by comparison, his siblings (for reasons unknown) did not. It is also more than a coincidence that both

Cleansman and Nixon achieved much more than other members of the family.

This entire situation sets up a dichotomy that could not have failed to plague young Richard Nixon. It must have given rise within him to significant feelings of uncertainty about himself as a person and, more specifically, as a male. As a male child in a family dominated by a female, Nixon apparently had the strongest identification with that female.

Feeling uncertain as a man

Before supporting and elaborating on the significance of this important constellation of identifications, some clarification is needed. By "identification" I refer to the highly complex process through which a child tends, unconsciously, to model himself after others. Children can identify with many people (e.g., a school teacher or a minister), but usually the primary objects of identification are parents.

It would be naive to say that Richard Nixon as a child identified *only* with his mother or *only* with his father; this would be all but impossible, since both of his parents were around during most of his childhood. It is more accurate to say that in some ways he seems to have identified with each of his parents, but *primarily* with his mother.

Mother was primary

Mazo's biography tends to support this dramatically. The fact that Nixon has fought tenaciously for success even after major failures further sustains this theory. The man has overwhelmingly subscribed to his mother's formulas for success; he has been almost a caricature of the work ethic in action.

I also hypothesize that Nixon had important identifications with his father, important enough to alter his mother's script of life somewhat. While she harbored some aspirations for Richard to join the clergy, the father's interest in politics and debate must have been a major influence on his son's career.

Fearing father's failure

Likewise, Richard Nixon, starting in his later college days, has at times departed dramatically from his mother's characteristic Quaker pacifism. Mazlish, in another vein, postulates some negative father identifications, especially with Frank Nixon's failure to achieve success; it is quite reasonable to consider that Nixon feared turning out the same way.

Of central importance is the question of how Richard Nixon as a child achieved a sense of masculinity in a household where Mother was the stronger of the two parents. We are accustomed, in our Occidental society, to consider strength and domination as masculine traits and weakness and submission as feminine. With the advent of women's liberation this stereotype is changing, but in early twentieth-century California the situation was very much in line with the stereotypical features.

We know from Mazo and others that Nixon was a child who tended toward submission; in today's culture we would describe him as going along with the establishment. Though it might be unfair to characterize him as a weak child, he certainly was not robust. From the time of the buggy accident at age three, in which he was almost killed, Nixon was susceptible to a variety of illnesses.

It is very important for me to emphasize at this point that young Richard was evolving as a somewhat insecure child who, with some reluctance, found himself submissive to a fear-inspiring father and, even worse, a dominating mother. We also see a sometimes sick child, who therefore has some question about his own sense of general physical security and masculinity. This problem is exacerbated by the child's identification with:

A vulnerable child

1. A powerful, ambitious, hardworking,

    dominating mother and maternal grand-
mother.

2. A relatively weak, unsuccessful, submissive father, whose ambitiousness was
pushed by his driving wife.

Young Nixon, growing up under this dichotomy, must have experienced considerable sexual confusion. In some very important ways,
the masculine and feminine roles of Mr. and
Mrs. Nixon were dramatically reversed, and
this problem had to be resolved by Richard and
his brothers. Practically speaking, there were
two ways for young Richard to solve his identification puzzle. He could have concluded:

1. Men are weak; women are strong.
Therefore, since I want to be strong, I
must gravitate toward femininity and
away from masculinity. I can then be
strong and secure like my mother.

or:

2. Men are weak, passive, and submissive.
Though I am a man, I will deny these
facts and become strong anyway.

Such scenarios are played out on the conscious but more especially on the unconscious level.

A child growing up guided by the first scenario will tend to be submissive, weak, possibly effeminate, and perhaps even homosexual.

By observing Richard Nixon, it can be said with confidence that he has not given in to the "strengths" and security of femininity. Nixon in every way is a picture of masculinity, at least as we see him today. But while he seems to have effectively resolved a significant sexual-identity riddle, he at one point demonstrated the existence of such a problem. I will begin to document this by analyzing another Mazo finding:

Solving the femininity problem

"He was a willing helper around the house when the chores were 'men's work.' But before submitting to tasks associated with girls, like washing the dishes, he would draw the blinds tight to shut the world out from his humiliation."

This again reminds us of the young boy's forced submission and introduces us to his overconcern with the important task of proving himself manly. A profound fear of being feminine (weak, submissive, sissyfied) best explains his excessive concern over being

Shutting out the world

humiliated and his resulting feeling that it was necessary to "shut the world out." This need eventually gave rise to Nixon's lifelong pattern of "shutting the world out," and for excellent reason: Unconsciously, he is *helpless, dominated, and weak.* This tendency, fostered early in life, helps to explain why Richard Nixon has remained so private a person while in public life; why he prizes privacy and secrecy. To this day he is still "drawing the blinds tight to shut the world out from his [ongoing] humiliation."

To a boy secure in his sense of manliness and general well-being, washing the dishes is an annoyance at worst. To young Richard Nixon it was tantamount to becoming female. The sexual ambivalence of our young subject was not only caused by insecure feelings: It was also a source of such feelings. The arc that completes a vicious circle was complete.

He submits to Pat Even though it is generally assumed (probably correctly) that Nixon's sexual identity is pretty healthy, there is evidence that in some ways he recapitulated the paradoxical female sexual dominance of his parents later in life. Mazo enlightens us via a description of Nixon's early social relationships with Pat.

The future President is described as having "hung around dutifully" waiting for Pat "even when she had other dates and would drive her to Los Angeles if she was to meet someone there, and wait around to take her home." Young Nixon acquiesced to Pat in other ways. He socialized with *her* group of friends and became "part of the group."

Repeatedly in *Six Crises* Nixon hails the comparative strengths of women in general. Following his defeat by Kennedy, he points out, his male supporters gave up on him quickly. Women throughout the country continued to give their undying support. In his view, they were stronger than the men and did not give up as easily. Nixon goes on to express the feeling that what one needs for a successful political campaign is a core of enthusiastic females.

In summary, Richard Nixon can be seen emerging from his childhood psychologically healthy but hardly unscathed. He is seen to be plagued with anxiety arising out of an uncertainty about his own view of himself as a man. The young man also seems to be bothered by unconscious self-doubts that suggest he might be submissive, as was customary for women at the time. Consequently we find the boy in a double bind.

Young Nixon's double bind

Even though we are aware of his endeavors to appear strong and dominating (as men are theoretically supposed to be), we are also aware of the built-in contradiction inherent in his family history. For if he emulates strength and domination, he is in fact emulating his mother, a woman. In other words, to be strong is to be womanlike.

Adding to this the earlier ingredients of frequent illnesses (and the buggy accident), the deaths of two brothers, and the two-year separation from his mother, we wind up with a picture of anxieties, confusions, and contradictions. These anxieties, confusions, and contradictions form the seeds of young Richard Nixon's powerful feelings of insecurity.

In the following sections we will trace the germination of these seeds into the mystery man under study here.

The war within Nixon

Watching Nixon emerge from childhood with a somewhat insecure personality foundation, it is fascinating to discover the incredibly elaborate system of man's compensatory supports. The series of psychic contradictions and confusions described in the preceding section sets the stage for an emotional battleground.

The inevitable outgrowth of emotional conflict is anxiety. Further examination will

reveal various conscious and unconscious com-
ponents of Richard Nixon's personality, warring with one another in a series of conflicts that
can never be solved. The fuel that feeds this
process is anxiety, which must be either dissipated or somehow contained. Eventually I
will show how the methods used by Nixon to
dissipate and control anxiety are responsible for
his overt behavioral characteristics.

While all of us experience anxiety in a multitude of forms, few people have been able to
harness this energy as effectively and efficiently
as Richard Nixon. This accounts for much of
this man's greatness as well as weakness, and
Nixon's anxieties and anxiety-containing
mechanisms will be studied here in this context.

Harnessing for greatness

The following unavoidable detour is a useful
prelude to this analysis. While attempting to
avoid a smokescreen of confusing technical
nomenclature, I wish to schematize some
general considerations about anxiety.

A most abstract concept, anxiety tends to
elude simplistic definition and is misunderstood
quite frequently. Some overt manifestations of
anxiety are so ubiquitous that they hardly need
to be mentioned: Everyone at times
experiences the rapid, pounding pulse, the
sweating, tremulousness, rapid breathing, and

stomach churnings that result from anxiousness. But the worst and most intolerable offshoot of anxiety is a feeling of vague impending doom, the feeling that something overwhelming and ghastly is about to happen.

What anxiety is To a certain degree the feeling resembles fear, but, unlike fear, anxiety is not experienced in connection with an external, realistic, conscious danger. For example, a passenger in an airplane that is about to crash certainly appears anxious, but, strictly speaking, he is frightened; the fact that momentary death might be evident explains the phenomenon. With anxiety, ominous feelings of doom are experienced but the actual threat of doom is not really present.

Anxiety probably begins soon after birth, and the production of it continues throughout life. The most important aspect of concern here is that no one can tolerate very much anxiety. Therefore, everyone intuitively (and unconsciously) learns to deal with it by using a variety of psychological mechanisms. These serve to protect one from the sense of doom and therefore act as a kind of defense; they are the so-called psychological mechanisms of defense. The theoretical foundation for these defense mechanisms was built by Sigmund Freud;

credit for the delineation of the specifics belongs largely to his daughter Anna.

Earlier I described a series of conflicts that must have confronted Richard Nixon during his childhood. Further clarification of these conflicts will explain some of the early probable sources of anxiety in our subject.

It is again necessary to focus on young Nixon's immersion into religious fundamentalism, logically beginning where the church itself often begins its childhood instruction, with the Ten Commandments. Consider first the commandment of "Honor your father and your mother," which is one of the few dictates written positively. (It does not contain "not.") Nevertheless, it probably symbolizes one of the greatest sources of conflict for young Richard.

Trouble with a Commandment

Taking into account the general Nixon family constellation, the church dictate assumes a much more sweeping meaning. In a more diffuse sense the command can best be interpreted to mean "Thou shalt love and honor thy parents and all other persons in authority." This injunction is further amplified by "You shall not take the name of the Lord your God in vain" because this really is a demand of unwavering respect for a more abstract authority, God.

That old-time fundamentalist flavor

It is quite safe to conclude from the research of the biographers that Hannah Milhous's Quakerism demanded stringent literal acquiescence to such unfaltering respect of all authority. This is suggested by the fact that Nixon's grandmother frequently used "plain speech." Mazo quoting Nixon: "She used the plain speech (thee and thou) exclusively. My mother used the plain speech in talking with her and her sisters, but never with the children." Since Nixon's maternal grandmother was a powerful family influence, the fact that she spoke exclusively in this Biblical phraseology again emphasizes the fundamentalist flavor of the young boy's environment.

Although Frank Nixon was certainly less religiously oriented, he nevertheless injected an overwhelming ingredient of authoritarianism into his son's early life. Adding Nixon's never-to-be-argued-with father to an atmosphere already containing the authority of his grandmother, mother, and church, we can conclude that, psychologically speaking, Nixon grew up in a kind of microcosmic "police state."

Functioning in a straitjacket

It is revealing to observe how the young boy functioned in this rigidly controlled emotional straitjacket. Drawing again on biographical material, we know he cooperated fully with this confining environment, only on occasion to be seen out of step. Even then "Richard took his spankings without a whimper" (Mazo).

Pitted against this emotionally constraining environment, we see a child who sometimes experiences ill feelings toward his parents as well as others in authority. On occasion he will have had aggressive impulses toward them: to injure them, replace them, or perhaps to wish tragedy upon them. We need only to acknowledge that Richard Nixon is a human being to infer this without question. We know that, with the possible exception of the profoundly mentally retarded child, children cannot *always* love, honor, respect, and obey parents. Such an ideal set of conditions *never* exists, simply because no parent can please his child all of the time and no child can be pleased all of the time. A child's needs are sometimes insatiable, and it is during such times that all children experience some feelings of rejection or resentment.

The preceding paragraphs describe two sides of a distressing conflict which must have been omnipresent for young Nixon:

1. I must always love, honor, respect, and

obey my parents. In addition, I must be careful not to disagree with them.

2. I do not always love, honor, respect, and obey my parents. In addition, at times I disagree with them.

No compromise with imperfections

Even though most children growing up in our culture today are exposed to the Ten Commandments and other forms of authoritarianism, they are not usually faced with this conflict in such a dramatic way. Parents who tend to be more open and flexible will at times allow their children the luxury of disrespect and disagreement. Likewise, most churches today are gravitating toward a more realistic, compromise-accepting approach to the imperfections of children. However, we are given ample evidence by Mazo and De Toledano that this was not the case for our young subject.

Nixon was unrelenting in his efforts to satisfy the varied demands of his parents and others. It is likely that as a child he even tried consciously to avoid thinking ill thoughts of his parents, the church, and the other controlling influences in his life. Although to an impressive degree he was outwardly able to live up to what are really superhuman expectations, he still had to deal simultaneously with his inevitable, merely human impulses, which sometimes went against the grain of the church, his mother, father, and grandmother. Whenever he was backed into a corner, he was almost totally without a safety valve through which to release some normal, human (but unpleasant) aggressive feelings.

The byproduct of this incessant conflict could only have been a significant burden of anxiety. The intolerable pressure of this anxiety could have been reduced only by resolving the conflict, the source of anxiety.

His anxiety increased

The direct approach—ventilation of the aggressive feelings—was out of the question for young Nixon, given his personality and the strict authoritarian setting within the home. I contend that Nixon's solution for this continuing conflict was to exclude certain elements of his dilemma from his awareness.

By making himself unaware of his negative feelings against his parents and other authorities, he was able to bury one side of the conflict. Having accomplished this, the conflict was neutralized.

What I have described is the mechanism known as repression. It is the most fundamental device utilized by the mind to resolve conflicts

The role of repression

and control anxiety. It is an automatic process by which uncomfortable memories, conflicts, and desires are excluded from awareness. They are not forgotten. Rather, they are accumulated and kept out of *conscious* awareness; they are, in other words, channeled into the *unconscious*, although they are not in a dormant state.

Throughout life these unconscious impulses continue to war with their conscious counterparts in attempts to emerge into awareness. So even though Nixon was known as a child to be quite submissive to those in authority, it is certain that he emerged from his childhood with an unconscious storehouse heavily laden with strong aggressive impulses.

Explosions are the outlet

Nixon's childhood rearing was a paradigm of the very kind of circumstances that encourage the need to repress an infinite number of impulses. While he remained submissive most of the time, there are clues that point to the presence of the ever threatening underlying pressures. One outlet for Nixon's pent-up feelings was to explode at someone. The explosions were infrequent but thorough-going. De Toledano quoting F. Donald Nixon, Richard's brother: "He wouldn't argue much with me but once, when he had just about as much of me as he could take, he cut loose and kept at it for a half hour. He went back a year listing things I had done. He didn't leave out a thing. I've had a lot of respect ever since for the way he can keep things on his mind."

Here is evidence that Nixon had a tendency to hold things back (repress) for long periods of time. He held back his anger over numerous "things" that Donald must have done to irritate him. But the anger was not dissipated; it was stored. Similarly, the irritating "things" were not forgotten; they were stored. At times Nixon's overloaded unconscious was unable to bear the strain and the stored aggressions were allowed to surface; then "he cut loose" and "didn't leave out a thing."

Though these rare explosions allowed some escape for Nixon's repressed impulses, they certainly fell short of ventilating his gigantic, tumultuous conflict with authority and aggression. For not only was Nixon frightened of authority: He was fearful of his own aggressive impulses, as demonstrated by Donald Nixon's example.

He feared his impulses

If Richard Nixon had not had an ongoing fear of his own unconscious aggressions, he would have been able to deal with his brother more directly on a day-to-day basis. This would have eliminated the need to save up these aggressions for such an explosive outburst. The fact that he needed o keep these impulses contained for so long provides strong evidence that Nixon fears his own aggressions.

When there is no acceptable way to vent such feelings outwardly, there remains only the one alternative: They must be turned inward, repressed. There is little question in my own analysis that Nixon's unconscious is a vault bulging with aggression. Later I will discuss the outlets and channelings for this aggression, and will document its existence further.

Milhous versus Nixon   Conflict gives rise to unharnessed unconscious aggressions; out of this aggression emerges new conflict. I have described the evolution of Richard Nixon's unconscious storehouse as well as some of the contents. Another early conflict that plagued Nixon from childhood through his political life was that of "Milhous versus Nixon." I refer again to the dichotomy of a powerful, dominating, yet pacifistic mother who was experienced by Richard along with an argumentative, punitive, hot-tempered, extroverted father.

Hannah Nixon was a gentle, peace-loving

woman even though she dominated the entire family, including her husband. Frank Nixon, though dominated by his wife, was a political reactionary, in the sense that he reacted dramatically to what he felt were political injustices; he was a fighter.

Earlier I referred to Nixon's identifications with his dominating mother and dominated father; at this point other aspects of the boy's parental identifications deserve examination. The dichotomy of this conflict is:

Pacifist mother, violent father

1. I am like my mother, a gentle pacifist.
2. I am like my father, an uncompromising reactionary.

It would be just about impossible for Nixon to live up to both of these standards simultaneously—they cannot coexist. This is a partial explanation for Nixon's puzzling patterns of ambivalence. I refer, for example, to a man whose reputation was built on a tough stance of anti-Communism, who later approached a hot war with the Communists as a hawk—but who, paradoxically, became the first U.S. President to meet with Mao Tse-tung for the purpose of peaceful conciliation.

The dove within the hawk

By repressing the Milhous identification, he is able to function smoothly as a war hawk. At other times he is a conscious Milhous, and shows it by way of his diplomatic missions designed as authentic strategy to achieve peace. In this parent-built paradox lies one of Nixon's greatest strengths and apparent flexibilities.

Because Nixon's primary identifications seem to be with his mother, he is able, most of the time, to keep the "Frank Nixon elements" repressed. Yet these elements continue to seek the light of day and at times come to the surface in the form of a surprising explosion.

That Manson slipup

A most classic and familiar example was the famous candid Nixon remark on August 3, 1970, about the Charles Manson murder trial. *Nixon in the White House* reports:

Charging that newspapers and television were glorifying Manson in their coverage of his trial in Los Angeles, Nixon blurted out, "Here is a man who is guilty, directly or indirectly, of eight murders without reason." Immediately afterward, Press Secretary Ron Ziegler tried to mitigate Nixon's blunder by saying, . . . "there is

no attempt to impute liability to any accused
(sic). *The gist of his statement was just the con-*
trary." ... *Not until that December 10 press*
conference, four months later, did the President
admit his offense, inexcusable for a lawyer.

And so, when Nixon is functioning as a
Milhous, the Nixon side will at times surface in
the form of gut reaction. But the converse set of
circumstances is probably a greater challenge
for the President. In the midst of crises over
such issues as busing, campus violence, drug
use, and communism we lose sight of Milhous
and see the Nixon elements emerging to the
forefront, the replication of a man who is
"never to be argued with."

An example of the uncompromising "Frank
Nixon element" is Nixon's behavior in connection with his abortive Supreme Court nominations. On August 18, 1969, Clement F. Hayns-
worth, Jr., was nominated, only to be rejected
on November 21. An outraged Nixon, refusing
to compromise, then nominated G. Harrold
Carswell (on January 19, 1970), who was
likewise defeated. Both men, Southern conser-
vatives, seemed to fit well into Nixon's scheme,
but not into the Senate's. My point is that even

Those abortive
Supreme Court
nominations

after the first rejection, Nixon, like his unyielding father, refused to give in to the face of reality.

When he is seen publicly during such crises, his voice is heard to quiver, and he appears most tense. He appears less comfortable as Nixon than as Milhous. Throughout the Watergate scandal Nixon has been forced into this same role, and the effects, to be detailed later, have been most threatening to him.

Up to now in this profile, I have attempted to convey primarily two pivotal postulations:

1. From his childhood Nixon has been a basically healthy person who at various levels, conscious and unconscious, senses and is affected by certain significant insecurities.
2. The rigidity of his emotional environment has contributed to the continued existence of an unconscious storehouse of powerful aggressive feelings.

Nixon the Nautilus   Richard Nixon's most highly organized and finely honed weapon against his underlying insecurities is his ability to maintain strenuous self-control. To document this aspect of the man, I have spent much time in close observation—once in person (during the 1968 campaign) but mostly via many hours of watching television interviews, speeches, and press conferences. In Nixon's conscious and unconscious strivings to isolate his inner self from observation, he unknowingly is most revealing.

Opening statements such as "Let me be perfectly clear," "Let me be quite candid," "Let me speak with candor," and "Let me make this point crystal clear" are long-familiar trademarks of the Nixon rhetoric. On the surface, such statements appear to be reasonable ways to initiate points, but the excessive usage of them indicates something more. A closer analysis permits at least two revealing conclusions.

At the risk of appearing politically naive, I will assume here that the public expects some emotional straightforwardness from a public official at a press conference. Everyone grants that no one can be totally honest all of the time; nevertheless, we do expect some candor in public colloquy. Similarly, the fact that a public official has been elected by the people should indicate a degree of mutual trust. Within that context such utterances as "Let me

"Let me be quite candid"

be quite candid" become unnecessary redundancies. A reasonable amount of candor should be taken for granted in the first place. While such assertions are really not required by the public, they are obligatory for Nixon. It is evident that he finds it indispensable continually to reemphasize his frankness.

It is quite possible that during a press conference Nixon sees himself as candid even when he is not; the reality is acknowledged only unconsciously. Because of the constant presence of these unconscious forces, Nixon tends to use such expressions automatically and liberally. He *needs* to use these expressions to convince himself of "truths" that he is uncertain about.

An obvious artifice The frequency of these pronouncements tends to undermine what the man is so desperately (and consciously) but ineffectively trying to do. While the phrase "being perfectly candid" provides some self-reassurance for its user, it tends to have an artificial sound to the ears of the listeners. The expressions can therefore be labeled unconscious derivatives. They are not directed at the public, which is turned off by them. They are, rather, directed to the speaker from within.

As a psychiatrist, I find that when I take a

history from a patient who employs excessive energy to defend his own credibility as a historian, rather than just *being* a historian, he is actually being less than candid. For example, during the course of an appointment John tells me that what he is about to say is "absolutely true." At this point I ask myself (and, if appropriate, I may ask John), "Why do you have to assure me of your veracity when I tend to assume it?" I find myself asking the same question about Richard Nixon. In his attempts to document his candor, he is demonstrating a lack of it.

Still another insight into Nixon lurks in his common expressions. The familiar statements about candor, crystal clarity, etc., are usually prefaced by "Let me," or "Allow me," or "With your permission." Superficially, one might look upon this locution as a diplomatic or courteous gesture, like saying "Pardon me, but . . ." Indeed, these are courteous expressions, expressions of submission. We recall that as a child Nixon was often forced into submission by a father who was "never to be argued with." Young Richard was usually able to repress his anger over this submission, and therefore sought and derived comfort from his passive stance.

When courtesy signifies submission

I believe that he approaches the press and the public, at least outwardly, much as he did his father. But inside there remains the repressed element of contempt for father, the press, etc. Occasionally this repressed element is blurted out. A famous example was Nixon's contemptuous statement to the press after his 1962 defeat in the California gubernatorial election that the reporters would no longer "have Dick Nixon to kick around."

He fears reporters' questions

During most sessions of public inquiry Nixon probably feels in control, and probably feels candid. But I believe it is an ongoing need to submit that causes him to open so many statements by asking permission. In reality he is quite afraid of his questioners. He is bowing to authority, begging for understanding, even praying for forgiveness in the event someone might (for example) disagree with him.

This is reminiscent of the conflict described earlier. Nixon is a man who needs to feel that he is in command. His continuing unconscious fear of reprisal from authority forces him to be humbling in his speech as well as in his behavior.

And so the phrase "Let me speak with candor" is a meager device that attempts to camouflage a man who is calculating and rigidly controlling, not candid. It is also a statement of humility for a man of apparent strength who fears his own inner sense of weakness.

Nixon's typical gestures offer another clue to his mysterious personality. The famous Nixonian arm movements resemble those of a robot and reflect their calculated nature. His back and trunk usually remain stiff. He moves like a cumbersome unitized structure. This appears to be the result of high muscle tone, which in turn reflects tension and control.

Robotized arm movements

His facial expressions do not come across with any degree of warmth or naturalness. The familiar pensive look is interrupted occasionally by a rapid, transient smile which switches on and off like a neon sign. Even during the momentary smile one gets the glimmer of an ambivalent clown face subtly frowning through a painted smile.

The ambivalent smile

The emotional tone of Nixon's voice covers a very limited range of inflection. It is perpetually businesslike. The sound of the infrequent laugh is forced and limited; it too echoes a businesslike quality. The President's serious, always professional and formally polished

The limited voice range

quality persists even on the golf course and in other situations where it is not demanded.

Why must this man so consistently display such an exaggerated measure of composure? As in the Steve Cleansman example, being in control is really an effort to ward off feelings of self-uncertainty. Unconsciously, Nixon is likely distressed by such feelings of being less than perfect, and this is a result of the factors described in the first sections of this chapter. Despite the presence of a surplus of unconscious insecurities, one can successfully deny the existence of those insecurities to oneself if one can achieve absolute control over oneself.

The payoff of absolute command

The need to be in absolute command arises partially out of an uneasiness over being commanded. Paraphrasing Leon Salzman: A person can try to achieve absolute control over all aspects of living by acquiring a knowledge of all possibilities in life that might occur. In addition to acquiring a knowledge of all possibilities in life, one must be *prepared* for all possibilities in life. In order to be constantly prepared, one must be in control of oneself at all times and must never let down one's guard.

Using these psychological mechanisms, Nixon has theoretically placed himself in a position of incredible power: He can anticipate and prepare for anything that might happen in his life!

While many people (especially successful achievers) operate to varying degrees on the same principle, there is ample evidence that Nixon has followed it as a psychological modus operandi, a law of life. A profusion of biographical and autobiographical data supports this important contention. From Evans and Novak: "For Nixon the politician, far more than Lyndon Johnson or John F. Kennedy or Dwight Eisenhower, concealed Nixon the man, and the man was, even to some of his close friends, an unbelievably complex, shy, remote and tense figure whose iron control seldom permitted anyone to glimpse the tumult inside."

The "submarine effect" described in the third chapter partially explains the evolution of Nixon's ways of achieving control. It also demonstrates how such control mechanisms evolve out of a need to avoid feelings of uncertainty. When one studies the Cleansman prototype silhouetted against Nixon's childhood insecurities, the metamorphosis of Nixon's personality becomes easier to follow. By observing the finished product (as Evans and Novak have, above) in conjunction with past history and the

Avoiding uncertainty

"Cleansman mechanisms," my findings become plausible.

Another Nixon-Cleansman correlation is the striking similarity in the way by which the two men pursue control. Steve's necessity for control arose out of self-uncertainty, and in given situations he strove desperately for total knowledge and perfection. By knowing everything and planning for everything, he was able to assume control over everything and, in turn, reduce feelings of uncertainty. This strikes a chord in Nixon's own approach to life.

That "passion for facts"

De Toledano reports: "In those boyhood days two aspects of ... the 'Nixon method' were already apparent. The first was a passion for facts. ... The second aspect of the 'Nixon method' was that Nixon has had an uncommon ability to take advantage of a situation before and after it develops. His success is due to knowing what to do and when to do it, perfect timing in everything."

While Nixon, then, has a "passion for facts," he is likewise passionate in his need to "take advantage of a situation," to have it under his total control. Our subject has a very real fear of leaving out any detail for fear he might overlook something important. An unfortunate aspect of this fear is that it can interfere with judgment. Overconcern with details can undermine one's perspective: If nothing is considered unimportant and everything is important, the mind can get bogged down with trivia.

Nixon illustrates this vividly in his description (in *Six Crises*) of the fateful 1960 campaign: "At 4:30 Sunday afternoon, we took off for Alaska, a trip which was to mark the fulfillment of the pledge, made in my acceptance speech, to carry the campaign into every one of the fifty states. Not even our most optimistic supporters thought we had a chance to carry Alaska."

Wild goose chase to Alaska

This accounting is revealing. First we get a sampling of Nixon's obsession with detail in his writing style: "4:30 Sunday afternoon"; the book is papered with such unneeded minutiae. More important, we see Nixon's obsession with detail on a much grander scale: He must campaign in every state, leave no stone unturned.

Politically such an all-inclusive crusade could not be justified. It was general knowledge that the election was pivoting on key precincts in Chicago and other large cities. The need to mount the trip to Alaska arose from neurotic necessity, not political need. Nixon himself tells us this indirectly by his admission of pessimism over carrying Alaska. The situation takes on even a greater level of political absurdity when one considers the number of hours spent traveling to the remote area and the number of electoral votes at stake.

Impaired judgment

The episode dramatizes Nixon's tendency toward overkill when he prepared to meet situations. He must do this to convince himself *unconsciously* that he is invulnerable, that he has done everything possible, covered every detail. In responding to these *unconscious* drives, he unfortunately shortchanges *conscious* judgments.

Another typical example of Nixon's obsession with detail impairing his good judgment can be found in his sixth crisis, the campaign of 1960. His hospital stay for a knee infection had left him with a huge backlog of paperwork, but even though his staff had sifted through (and essentially handled) all the material, Nixon felt that it was *his* responsibility to "review each answer in detail." This was early in the campaign, and there is little question that Nixon could have made much better use of his time than redoing routine paperwork.

The payoff of neurosis

I am confident that Nixon's neurotic need to know all and do all has provided the fuel that won his debates in school, maintained his law scholarship, and propelled his ascent in politics. Maintaining control of everything seems to have been a lifelong obsession for Nixon, and his quest for a self-sufficient iron-clad utopia has not been without other advantages.

During Nixon's 1959 Moscow meeting with Nikita Khrushchev, the Communist leader surprised the Vice-President with some unanticipated profanities. Nixon describes his reaction: "His attack at this early stage of my visit had been a surprise. His vehemence and choice of language had been a shock. But my intense preparation for the visit and my study of his past tactics helped me to meet his attack without losing my temper or my sense of balance."

Nixon's preparation for the semi-summit was most impressive (if not a case of overkill), and perhaps it did help him to maintain a "sense of balance." But it also permits additional insight into Nixon.

We learn that Richard Nixon does not like surprises; Khrushchev's assault had broken the bonds of the usually stuffy, formalized diplomacy. Khrushchev was shooting from the hip, speaking with candor. The real shock for Nixon could not have been the profanities. (Nixon is a former Navy man.) It was the unexpected frankness.

Unexpected frankness hurts

Candor demands candor; the fact that

Khrushchev was behaving as he did put a demand on Nixon that he likewise be candid. This was not a high school debate or press conference; there were no carefully planned rules. The frankness of the situation posed a tremendous problem to this man of composure and preplanning. Candor was the one thing Nixon could not preplan; in fact, if one tries to plan candor, the results tend to backfire.

Why Khrushchev shocked Nixon

Nixon's need to explain how he avoided losing his temper and balance shows that he found it necessary to prevent this from occurring. For Nixon, losing control would have been tantamount to demise. So it becomes obvious why the situation was experienced as a shock. How does one react to candor when one is too controlled to be candid? Even though Nixon did not lose his temper, he did certainly lose control of the situation. Therein lies the "shock."

It really does not matter whether we consider lack of candor and spontaneity in the context of a top-level meeting or in a trivial situation; the principles are the same. Borrowing from Evans and Novak:

Often the precise idiom or choice of words to make a point or to make an apt response seemed just beyond the President's grasp. . . . During his campaign in St. Petersburg, Florida, in October 1970, a motorcycle policeman was thrown from his vehicle in the Presidential caravan and severely injured. . . . Nixon rushed to the injured policeman and expressed his sympathies. The policeman replied that he was sorry that the motorcade had been delayed. Then, embarrassing silence—the President speechless for seconds. Finally he blurted out: "Do you like the work?"

Hardly a sympathetic comment appropriate to the occasion.

Total control of personality cannot coexist with candor or a sense of humor or spontaneity. The last three traits require a certain amount of comfort with oneself, and this comfort Richard Nixon cannot afford psychologically. If he were able to loosen his guard enough to take on candor or humor, he would be relinquishing the important controls that keep him afloat. Steve Cleansman's reaction to surprise (being thrown into the shower) helps to explain the complicated dynamics that shocked (or silenced) Nixon in the two preceding incidents.

Again like Cleansman, Nixon has no sense of humor but enjoys a practical joke; the joker

The dangers of humor

cannot tolerate being the jokee. Novak and Evans document this: "His lack of wit and humor was a cliché both in and outside the White House, but he was capable of practical jokes of a rather high order. . . . He ordered the White House police force to wear elegant ceremonial uniforms like the household guard in a European court . . . the costumes unleashed a public torrent of abuse, and the President quickly retreated." It is noteworthy that the joke involved the humiliation of the "palace guards" at the hands of someone behaving like a pompous medieval king. The similarity between this and the Cleansman dynamics is apparent.

Nothing must be overlooked   Nixon's paramount dread is that he might overlook something and therefore commit an error. This is equivalent to complete failure for our man, who (like Steve Cleansman) sees everything important in his life as an all-or-nothing proposition; a job is either done perfectly or it is done poorly, a failure.

Mistakes are intolerable, a point that Nixon beats to death in *Six Crises:* "The point of greatest danger is not during the battle itself, but in the period immediately after. . . . Then, completely exhausted and drained emotionally, he must watch his decisions carefully. Then there is an increased possibility of error because he may lack the necessary cushion of emotional and mental reserve which is essential for good judgment."

This not only demonstrates an obsession to keep up an emotional guard. It also testifies to the tremendous energy that is required to keep control. It is no accident that Nixon's crises go on and on. He tends to view life as a series of battles. Six of them are described in his 1962 book, but more must be fought continually. Though he is always able to find an external enemy, more significant war is being waged on Nixon's internal battlefield. (The warring factions were introduced previously.)

The high price of control

Nixon himself is sometimes aware of the battle fatigue, though he seems out of touch with the internal battle locale: "Holding back when you have something you want to say is far more wearing on the system than letting yourself go." One is entitled to wonder whether Nixon, in this observation from *Six Crises,* is unknowingly defining the ill effects of his own massive repression.

Despite such exhaustive efforts to maintain rigid self-control, even Richard Nixon (like Steve Cleansman) on occasion is unable to regulate himself. When by chance there is a slip

Slipups must be denied

of control, this is so alien to the man that he must deny it.

Denial is a psychological defense mechanism that functions to protect one from the obvious but undesired and often threatening implications that emerge from a particular situation. In Nixon's own account of a heated conversation with Khrushchev he says: "To some it may have looked as though we had both lost our tempers. But exactly the opposite was true. I had full and complete control of my temper and was aware of it."

If Nixon really felt he had not lost his temper, why did he suppose "it may have looked as though we had"? Why does he find it necessary to speak of his self-control in a superlative way, saying that *"exactly* the *opposite* was true" and that he had *"full* and *complete control"*?

"Protesting too much"   "Thou doth protest too much." By going to extremes to deny reality, he grants yet another insight for analysis. (The importance of Nixon's use of denial will be highlighted in the later discussion of the Watergate phenomenon.)

Nixon has gleaned from others the price that is paid for loss of control. At one point during the Alger Hiss investigation Hiss lost his temper. Nixon comments: "With his temper no longer under control, he did not fight as skill-fully as he did before." He even describes Hiss in this context as "fighting like a caged animal." It becomes evident that while Nixon must maintain total control, he delights in seeing an opponent out of control. His own mortal fear of losing control puts him in tune with the sense of power one can derive from being in control of someone who is out of control.

In *Six Crises* we are also delivered a direct insight into Nixon's mortal fear of losing control thanks to candor. In his description of admiration for Thomas Dewey, Nixon describes the man's candor in the context of its most devastating consequences: "This candor on Dewey's part probably lost him some friends in the political world, but I respected and admired him for it." In the succeeding sentence he relates how Dewey's Presidential defeat to Truman was a great loss.

Mortal fear of candor

The second thought follows the first directly; it appears to be a non sequitur unless the reader infers a cause-and-effect relationship between the two statements. It is apparent that Nixon is (unconsciously) blaming Dewey's candor for the narrow Presidential defeat. We know from observation that Nixon is not about to make the same mistake if he can help it.

On the other hand, Nixon also directly envies Dewey (as he later does Khrushchev), because Nixon would like to be candid—if he only could.

The inner life is off limits

In summary, one important psychological mechanism used by Nixon to ward off anxiety is to control himself and not allow anyone a look at his inner life. By constantly planning and preparing, he attempts to control every aspect of his future and tries to provide for every possible uncertainty. By doing so he wards off the anxieties associated with the unknown and accomplishes impressive amounts of work.

He is like a submarine or nautilus lurking about in the fluidity of his own mind. He is protected by a solid shell. No one can sight him except on occasion, when he inadvertently surfaces.

Nixon: the ambivalent anti-Communist

For almost half his life Richard Nixon has been a symbol of anti-Communism; in fact, his hard-line stance against Marxism (especially his participation in the Alger Hiss case) rocketed Nixon to national prominence in 1948, when he was only a thirty-five-year-old Congressman. To quote Nixon *(Six Crises):* "The Hiss case was the first major crisis of my political life. My name, my reputation and my career were ever to be linked with decisions I made and the actions I took in that case. . . ."

Then serving on the House Un-American Activities Committee, Nixon was helping to investigate Alger Hiss, a highly regarded former State Department official who was tied to the American Communist movement. Nixon could rightly lay claim for a great deal of credit in the investigation, which led to a conviction. Hiss served three years and eight months in prison.

Three of Nixon's Six Crises deal directly with his personal confrontations with the Communist enemy: the Alger Hiss Case, the ill-fated diplomatic visit to Caracas, Venezuela, and the face-to-face Moscow meeting with Nikita Khrushchev. Each of these occurrences, interestingly enough, gives the reader insight into Nixon's personality and his ambivalence toward Communism.

Three crises

In his own account of the Alger Hiss case he reveals an extraordinary fear and hatred of the American Communist movement: "In the years ahead I would never forget that where the battle against Communists is concerned, victories are never final so long as Communists are still able to fight.... In the Hiss case ... we followed methods with which few objective critics could find serious fault.... In dealing with Communists, any other procedure can play into their hands and usually does."

In these and related passages Nixon exudes a phobia that resembles a fear of wild animals —all of which must be eradicated lest they otherwise attack.

A phobic commitment

It is certainly reasonable that a U.S. citizen, especially one in politics, might be fearful of Communism and regard it with disgust. Realistically, Communism has at times posed a variety of threats to our way of life. But the extraordinary hatred displayed by Nixon causes me to ask: How does one become so totally committed and outspoken against such an amorphous enemy?

It does not seem possible to attribute Nixon's fervor to any personal involvements with this enemy early in his life. His parents did not have to flee Communists. He never had to fight in a war against Communists. Nor was he (in his own opinion) ever an expert on Communism. Further study makes plain that Nixon's abhorrence of this enemy does not stem from extrinsic causes. It arises from within. A subtle hint in that direction is concealed in the following autobiographical passage:

A malignant attitude

"What I shall try to do in these pages is to tell it as I experienced it—not only as an acute personal crisis but as a vivid case study of the continuing crisis of our times, a crisis with which we shall be confronted as long as aggressive international Communism is on the loose in the world."

This suggests a malignant, totally intolerant attitude which does not mesh well with the thoughts expressed on other subjects in Nixon's writing and rhetoric. We are also informed that the threat of Communism is not just an international crisis but a *personal* crisis. But we are not told here why Communism should be regarded as such an "acute" personal crisis.

Section five of *Six Crises* describes Nixon's meeting with Nikita Khrushchev in Moscow during the summer of 1959. It was during my analysis of this chapter that I became most impressed by the remarkable words of my hypothetical patient. The context of the Nixon-Khrushchev get-together demonstrates the unfolding of a most dramatic paradox. The first clue can be found by carefully analyzing what Nixon tends to observe in his hated Communist enemy, Khrushchev.

Nixon describes how "Khrushchev never plays by the rules. He *delights* in doing the unexpected." While his appraisal of the Marxist leader is accurate, it is interesting to keep in mind that Richard Nixon, a me-

When the opposition ignores the rules

ticulously controlled person, also delights in doing the unexpected. His trip to China, preceded by Henry Kissinger's unexpected trip, are outstanding examples of such moves, and he savored their success with pride. Evans and Novak tell us: "Richard Nixon himself was pleased with his coup. It had all the ingredients that Nixon liked most: surprise, novelty, shattering of precedence, high-level international politics."

Since Nixon himself loves the unexpected, I interpret his quote about Khrushchev's "delight" as substantial self-identification.

Nixon also describes a pleasant Sunday morning spent at Khrushchev's summer home: "as luxurious an estate as any I had ever visited. I could not help but think that the old Bolsheviks had come a long way since the days of their revolution." It is most apparent that Nixon envies Khrushchev for such an impressive possession, something greatly desired by the young Vice-President of modest means. The fact that Nixon was eventually to acquire two impressive estates of his own lends particular significance to his envious reaction.

A self-revel-ation   A few pages later, Nixon provides the reader with an "insight into Khrushchev" which, ironically, provides a cornerstone of understanding not of Khrushchev but rather of Nixon.

We [Nixon and Khrushchev] sat down to lunch with our wives at a long table set up on the lawn. . . . It was then that I got some further insight into Khrushchev's habits—and his essential nature as a cold, calculating, self-controlled tactician. . . . He hardly touched the array of vodka and wine bottles. . . . His famed temper is always his servant and not his master, his drinking is strictly for pleasure and is never permitted to interfere with business. He was stone sober throughout our long afternoon of talks.

This is perhaps one of the most self-revealing statements in Nixon's book. While it is meant to describe Khrushchev only, it is also faithfully autobiographical. Nixon is the paragon of a "self-controlled tactician." As I have shown, self-control is an exceedingly important characteristic that defends the integrity of this man's underlying insecurities. At some level (probably unconscious for the most part) Nixon is aware of the importance of control, and so he admires his own familiar characteristic in his supposed enemy.

He envied Khrushchev

Nixon has been described by numerous biographers as "cold" and "calculating"—a personality characteristic that is in evidence whenever he makes a public appearance. During such occasions he is a caricature of a cold calculator. And so Nixon is admiring his own traits as, unconsciously, he sees them in Nikita Khrushchev.

Most noteworthy is his envy of Khrushchev's command over emotion—another overriding aspect of Nixon's own personality: He has absolute control over all emotional flow. Nixon speaks here of emotions acting as one's "servant" rather than as one's "master." This describes Nixon's would-be perversion of emotion. He regards emotion as though it were something to be used, like a utensil. In reality, emotions are simply experienced, not utilized.

The next Nixonian appraisal of Khrushchev offers even more autobiographical insight. Continuing his analysis of Khrushchev, Nixon writes:

A case of idol worship

"Intelligence, a quick hitting sense of humor, always on the offensive, colorful in action and words, a tendency to be a show-off, particularly where he has any kind of gallery to play to, a steel-like determination coupled with an almost compulsive tendency to press an advantage ... prides himself on knowing as much about his opponent's position as he does his own."

Here Nixon's unconscious envy of Nikita Khrushchev borders on idol worship; in fact, it resembles Nixon's idolizing of former Attorney General John Mitchell, which I will describe later.

The "tendency to be a show-off" in crowds has become a familiar Nixon trademark over the years. He frequently rushes into a group of cheering supporters for handshaking, followed by a seemingly surprised entourage of Secret Service men.

The presidential show-off

The phrase "steel-like determination" describes the Hannah Milhous work ethic that propelled Nixon from Yorba Linda to the White House. The "compulsive tendency to press an advantage" is something long ago mastered by Nixon.

Most transparent is Nixon's observation that Khrushchev "prides himself on knowing as much about his opponent's position as he does his own." Here the familiar submarine effect of Steve Cleansman is brought to light again. To reiterate: It is already clear that Nixon fends off unconscious insecure feelings by acquiring knowledge, accounting for every detail, preparing for every possible would-be occurrence.

"Preparing for battle"

The fact that Nixon is really talking about his own attributes *(and not necessarily Communist Khrushchev's attributes!)* is made obvious by the extent of the preparations which the future President made prior to his encounter with Khrushchev in 1959:

"In preparing for battle I have always found that plans are useless, but planning is indispensable. . . . For months before the trip I spent every spare moment studying. . . . I sought out men who had studied Soviet affairs and men who had met Khrushchev. . . . I was confident that I was better prepared than for any challenge I had faced in my entire life."

Nixon is obviously taken in by the admirable characteristics of his Communist enemy. His preparations for this relatively unimportant meeting can again be interpreted as a case of overkill, another compulsive attempt to achieve that total knowledge which supposedly provides total defense against all unknown anxieties.

Envy turned into jealousy

What of Nixon's reference to "a quick hitting sense of humor" and "colorful in actions and words"? Here envy escalates and turns into jealousy. He begrudges Khrushchev something that is unobtainable for Nixon: the ability to keep in total control while maintaining a sense of humor.

We have arrived at a potentially confusing crossroad. How does a man obsessed by the evils of Communism speak so highly (and show so much envy) of a major Communist world leader? Can this be the same Richard Nixon who spoke so venomously of Alger Hiss? The answer can be found in Richard Nixon's unconscious storehouse of difficult-to-deal-with impulses.

Earlier I mentioned that Nixon, as a child, began a lifelong process of accumulating these impulses, and that these materials cannot lie dormant. They are like radioactive waste products that can be dumped into the ocean or buried, but still continue to release energy.

One way to dissipate these unconsciously repressed elements is to project them outward and then attach them to someone else. This defines the psychological defense mechanism known as projection. Like the other defense mechanisms, projection operates unconsciously and automatically. It is an efficient and comfortable way for the mind to dispel alien, repressed feelings that give rise to intolerable anxiety.

What to do with repressed thoughts

For example, a person who has an inward fear of being homosexual can deny it and direct it outward. Perhaps he insists that his boss is homosexual and that this prevents him from getting a promotion. He also blames "homos" for "the deteriorating moral fiber of society."

Wanted: scapegoats Projection provides—in fact it demands—the existence of a scapegoat. Witness: "The Catholics are overpopulating the world," "The Blacks are trying to contaminate the white race through intermarriage," "The Jews won't be satisfied until they own the country."

In its most perverted form, projection can become an organized institution for inadequate people who are desperately looking for something to which they can attach (project) their own insecurities. The Ku Klux Klan and Nazism are horrifying cases in point.

What about Communism as a scapegoat? It seems evident to me that the John Birch Society, a figurehead of anti-Communism, is not anti-Communist because of altruism or patriotism but "projectionism." It allows members to attach their own undesirable feelings and characteristics onto an enemy (the Communists). Everything can be blamed on the Communists: drugs, aggression, immorality, fluoridation, and perhaps gonorrhea. This is massive projection at work.

How can it be explained that Richard Nixon is an avid anti-Communist even though he harbors obvious unconscious admiration for certain Communist strengths? (Up to now I have discussed only unconscious admiration of Khrushchev. Later, Nixon's admiration for general Communist principles will be delineated.) Can it be based upon his expertise on the subject, a thorough awareness of what results from Communism? Nixon himself rules this out by admitting (in *Six Crises*) that he is not such an expert. Mazlish also points to this fact in his Nixon inquiry.

Admiring Communist strengths

The collective answer or solution to this puzzle lies in Nixon's abundant use of projection and consequent scapegoating of Communists.

Another statement from *Six Crises* demonstrates how close Nixon actually comes to gaining insight into his own unconscious projections. Speaking of his 1958 confrontation in Caracas, Nixon comments, "When there is an obsession for maintaining order, freedom suffers; but without some order there can be no freedom."

"Order" is admired

In the first part of the statement he is speaking of centralized governmental suppression, such as occurs in Communist regimes, but in the light of my observations earlier it becomes apparent that the "obsession for maintaining order" is not only a classic Communist characteristic: It is a Nixon characteristic.

For our meticulous, perfectionistic subject, everything must be in its exact place; order equals security. Order and control are lifelong patterns for this man, who grew up in an emotional "police state" and whose primary campaign issues were the maintenance of law and order at home as well as abroad (e.g., Southeast Asia). Compared to the riots, protest marches, and other disruptions that tend to occur in the United States, the well-established Communist states are paradigms of law and order.

The shoe fits

I contend that Nixon secretly (perhaps mostly unconsciously) greatly envies this degree of Communist orderliness. It fits well into his compulsively organized personality structure. But while he envies this governmental system that best fits his personality structure, he cannot allow himself consciously to acknowledge that alien thought.

In the light of what I called "the war within,"

we are also aware of highly aggressive impulses that reside within Nixon's unconscious storehouse. Just as Nixon cannot consciously acknowledge an unconscious love of Communist-style order, he must likewise deny these lifelong pent-up unconscious aggressions. He deals with both of these sets of impulses by projecting them outward onto his scapegoat: Communism.

Harboring these alien, secret (unconscious) thoughts, he must keep them from emerging into consciousness; after all, Nixon is an American, and this implies a disgust for Communism and aggression. In order to fend off these impulses from within, he projects them externally; he becomes a powerful anti-Communist.

How Nixon became anti-Communist

This entire process is complicated and involves many defense mechanisms in addition to projection. For the sake of clarity I will not itemize every trivial aspect of this overall personality dynamic; the general concepts would then be lost in a matrix of detail. But one additional mechanism must be defined.

Like all the other defense mechanisms I have described, reaction formation operates beyond one's awareness—unconsciously. It is another device used by the unconscious to handle unacceptable thoughts or impulses. It is a mechanism of opposites; one goes to an opposite extreme to compensate for one's particular unacceptable impulses. For example, John unconsciously despises his sister. Because this is unacceptable, John always goes out of his way to be extra kind to her.

How reaction formation works

Before Nixon can bring the defense mechanism of projection to bear upon his unconscious affinity for Communism, he must alter his feelings of affinity. Using reaction formation, he can consciously dislike Communism. It now becomes possible for him to project his unconscious feelings of aggression and hate (originally meant for his parents, etc.) onto the Communists. Since hating parents is unacceptable and hating Communists is acceptable, this set of mechanisms channels anxiety, anger, and hatred in acceptable ways. In the event that this might appear somewhat complicated, the diagram on the facing page outlines this most important chain of psychological maneuvers.

The disguise drops

This is how Nixon can tack his uncomfortable unconscious thoughts onto a conscious enemy. (Mazlish previously suggested a similar set of mechanisms, but much more speculatively.)

At times Nixon's repressed thoughts show

Repressed Positive Feelings	Repressed Aggressive Feelings (Since Childhood)
I love the orderliness, etc., of Communism. I also greatly admire some Communist leaders, eg. Khrushchev.	I have always had some <u>aggressive</u> <u>hateful</u> feelings toward my mother, father, self, and many others who have been in authority over me.

<u>REACTION FORMATION</u>

PROJECTION

Altered Formerly Positive Feelings

I don't like the orderliness, etcetera, of Communism. I also don't admire some Communist leaders, eg. Khrushchev.

<u>UNCONSCIOUSNESS</u>

<u>CONSCIOUSNESS</u>

Communists are <u>aggressive</u> and <u>hateful</u>. I deplore Communism and <u>hate</u> their leaders.

themselves in relatively undisguised form. At least one section of *Six Crises* provides a clear window into Nixon's unconscious admiration for Communism:

> *The question was one of determination, of will, of stamina, of willingness to risk all for victory. How did we stack up against the kind of fanatically dedicated men I had seen in the past ten days [while visiting the U.S.S.R.]?*
>
> *I thought how ironical it was that the Communist leaders were getting more production out of their people by special incentives. In a nation which supposedly is guided by the philosophy of "everyone receives according to his needs and produces according to his ability," the disparity between the amounts paid more efficient workers and those who are less efficient is far greater than in the United States.*

The irony that wasn't

Here we can see Nixon struggling with a powerful challenge. His repressed admiration for Communism is threatening to break through the surface. In fact, in subtle ways it has broken through. Again, Nixon all but gains insight into his repressions, reaction formations, and projections. But he is able to rationalize them away as "ironical," which they are not.

Richard Nixon's unconscious sense of self-uncertainty and the unconscious mechanisms he uses to conceal (or otherwise deal with) these anxieties have served in many ways to buttress his substantial mental stability.

Nixon the decision maker

His tendency to overprepare has made him a master of political capability and diplomatic awareness. He is almost always well-researched, and exhibits an impressive ability to recall detail.

Despite (or perhaps because of) his lack of candor, he tends to be a genius of interpersonal diplomacy and an expert in his forte—foreign affairs.

Even his hidden aggressions have been channeled in a positive way through his fight against Communism.° The probable fact that his anti-Communist feelings might be uncon-

---

°I am not passing judgment on the value of Nixon's fight against Communism. But, psychologically speaking, his discharge of aggression onto the Communists is a socially acceptable, psychologically healthy means of dissipating anxiety.

scious projections does not detract from his accomplishments.

Errors are perceived as weakness

A negative side effect of Nixon's coping mechanisms is his frequent dysfunctioning in decision making. This series of mechanisms has been outlined in the Steve Cleansman prototype. The difficulty encountered in effecting decisions seems based upon a fear of not making the best possible choice or of committing a downright error. Any wrongful judgment represents a threat to integrity and exposes Nixon to a hint of inner weakness.

This threatened feeling appears to characterize Nixon's customary tightrope-walking approach to the making of even some minor decisions. Often he chooses to avoid acting, thereby eliminating the possibility of erring and consequent self-exposure.

A fear of decisiveness

In Nixon's notes (*Six Crises*) on the 1960 campaign, he accentuates the inherent dangers that result from making decisions. He displays his fear of decisiveness indirectly by considering some of the relative advantages of his opponent, John F. Kennedy. Nixon elaborates how his Vice-Presidential decision-making experiences could be a liability in the campaign against Kennedy:

"To gain experience, a man must make decisions. And when he makes decisions, he makes enemies. Then too, he must assume responsibility for the consequences of those decisions."

Here Nixon equates decision making with enemy making. He demonstrates the anguish he must experience often, whenever it becomes necessary to make a new enemy (decision). Certainly his statement is hyperbole but, based upon his underlying exaggerated fear of making a mistake (or, in this case, an enemy), decision making tends to provide a threat for this man, because *psychologically he cannot afford to be wrong.*

Decisions mean making enemies

Nixon goes on to describe how Kennedy was put in a position of advantage by being relatively inexperienced and having therefore made few decisions. Nixon complains that "there was very little . . . to shoot at."

Here is an example of how Kennedy could take advantage of the "submarine effect"; no one (including Nixon) could "shoot at" a past record of ill-fated Kennedy executive decisions, for none could be brought into view. Nixon, on the other hand, having served two terms as Vice-President, could not submerge. He was forced into view and into vulnerability.

Nixon's lack of self-confidence is also show-

A lack of self-confidence

ing here. He seems to overlook the obvious advantages of an incumbent, who (self-confidence permitting) can point with pride to the strengths that he has had ample occasion to display during his decision-making career.

In his treatment of the Alger Hiss case in *Six Crises*, Nixon also emphasizes his agony over decisions. At one phase in the investigation Nixon was compelled to decide whether or not to press on with the unpopular (and therefore politically risky) Hiss inquiry. Nixon's fear of a wrong decision makes him doubt his own judgment. The dread of not making the best possible decision feeds the always lingering unconscious doubts he has about himself in general. Approximately six pages are taken up with an explanation of his systematic but reluctant approach at making the final decision.

He begins: "Making the decision to meet a crisis is far more difficult than the test itself. One of the most trying experiences an individual can go through is the period of doubt. . . . It is in such a period that almost unbearable tensions build up."

The dread of being wrong

Nixon is saying that the *decision* to go ahead with investigation is more trying than the actual conduct of the investigation. This elucidates his ultimate dread of being proven wrong, something not tolerated by one who seeks security in being right. If Nixon's ultimate decree to proceed had led to a failure to convict Hiss, political embarrassment would have resulted. The fact that justice would have occurred anyway was of secondary importance; being in the right was paramount.

Along with choosing to continue the investigation, Nixon needed to guarantee a favorable outcome for himself. It was not enough to risk a decision to investigate Alger Hiss. Nixon required insurance that his decision would be equivalent to a prediction. In Nixon's mind, vindication for Hiss would be tantamount to personal failure. Justice is one thing. Being proven wrong spells doom.

The exaggerated importance that Nixon places on decision making seems partially related to the exaggerated importance that the man places on himself. A matter may lie beyond his control, yet he assumes personal responsibility. He viewed the possible outcomes of the Hiss case as reflections upon himself; realistically, they must be looked at as reflections on Hiss's guilt or innocence, not on Nixon's investigation.

Unrealistic feelings of responsibility

To illustrate: Jim, after some vacillation, decides to wash his car. Soon after there is an unanticipated cloudburst and the car is covered with water spots. Jim feels that he has failed by having made the decision to wash his car. Somehow he feels responsible for the cloudburst—which is hardly realistic.

Doubts, doubts and more doubts

Before Nixon decided to proceed with the Hiss inquiry, excessive doubting of his own judgment led him to solicit endless advice from colleagues. In roughly eight days he consulted Bert Andrews (of the New York *Herald-Tribune*), William Rogers (then chief counsel for a Senate subcommittee), Charles J. Kersten (congressman from Wisconsin), John Foster Dulles, and Allen Dulles. Even after unanimous opinions fron these respected confidants, Nixon persisted: "Still I was not satisfied."

At this point Nixon reinterrogated the star witness in the case, Whittaker Chambers. Then, continuing to doubt his own judgment, he asked Bert Andrews to accompany him on yet another interview at the home of witness Chambers. Still troubled by insatiable doubts and lack of self-confidence, Nixon recruited yet another colleague, Bob Stripling, for a final session in Chambers's home. Nixon refers to this last redundant meeting as his "final test."

Endless vacillation

This lengthy, even boring scenario supplies perspective for the inordinate self-doubting that Nixon experiences when he is in the throes of making a judgment; it also demonstrates the exaggerated fear he experiences in reaching a verdict. Like so many others with this difficulty, Nixon appears to vacillate endlessly between the alternatives of a resolution until time runs out. Time then forces him to decide impulsively.*

Nixon's account of the Hiss case dwells on his torment: "A leader is one who has the emotional, mental and physical strength to withstand pressures and tensions created by necessary doubts and then, at the critical moment, to make a choice and to act decisively. The men who fail are those who are so overcome by doubts that they either crack . . . or flee. . . ."

Nixon is straightforwardly conceding that "pressures and tensions" result from his tremendous self-doubting. He rationalizes away these doubts by labeling them as "necessary."

When he speaks of acting decisively "at the critical moment," he is avoiding what appears to be the reality of the situation. The "critical

The "critical" moment

---

*The reader may wish to refer back to the Steve Cleansman prototype to clarify the genesis of this difficulty.

moment" was actually forced upon him by his own prolonged doubting, vacillation, and procrastination. As time was running out, the "critical moment" was really nothing but the *last* moment.

To Nixon, *all* decisions, no matter how trivial, are unconsciously important decisions: They serve as an unconscious source of increased or decreased self-confidence, depending upon the outcome. Therefore, *no* decision can be unimportant. This explains Nixon's general fear of overlooking even the most trivial detail. After all, it just conceivably might prove important.

An excess of superlatives

Throughout Nixon's writings one also notices an excessive use of superlatives in describing his major speeches and decisions. Almost every campaign speech takes on a unique importance or is termed one of the best speeches of his career. Fearing that he might mistakenly leave out something that could be prominent, Nixon places importance on everything, especially decisions.

Nixon's own account of his concession speech to Kennedy in the 1960 election is a case in point. While the election was close in terms of the popular vote, there was general agreement that evening that Kennedy had won. The concession speech to Kennedy could be considered little more than a diplomatic ritual.

If Nixon had still thought he had a chance to win the election—by recounts, late absentee votes, etc.—he would not have considered making such a speech at all. Despite the inconsequence of the speech, Nixon in *Six Crises* again agonizes over it, and labels the event a major crisis. He compares it to the "Checkers" speech, his press conference following President Eisenhower's stroke, and his meeting with Khrushchev.

He then proclaims: "I had a split-second to decide whether to remain silent, to retreat, or to fight back."

The Checkers "Crisis"

What did Nixon mean by "fight back"?

It seems that he viewed the ritualistic concession speech as a potential battleground, not the benign formality that it really was. So he began what could have become endless vacillation and procrastination: "At least a dozen times I jotted down notes—and then tore the pages from the pad and tossed them in the waste basket."

In this case Nixon was unable to be decisive at all; after continued vacillations, he was forced by circumstances to make the speech on impulse: "I still had not been able to put down a note that I felt would be appropriate when Don Hughes opened the door and walked in, with Pat beside him." At this point Nixon was forced by his own procrastination to perform on impulse.

The process itself is the problem

Considering the relative unimportance of that speech, Nixon's vacillations appear to be much to do about nothing. But it is not the content of a decision that challenges Nixon so dramatically. It is the decision-making process itself.

The only way to absolutely avoid a poor decision is to put it off—only then one is forced to act quickly. This explains why Nixon is so logical and calculating on the one hand but unpredictable on the other. *The forced impulsivity accounts for the unpredictability.*

The evolution of Nixon's marital plans illustrates some aspects of this paradox. After Nixon had dated one girl (Ola Florence Welch) for a period of six years, he impulsively proposed to Pat on their first meeting. Though his decision to marry seemed somewhat impulsive, his choosing of an engagement ring was not. According to an article *(Time,* September 17, 1973), Nixon "kept Don [his brother] up half the night talking about the types of engagement rings that he had diligently investigated."

This typifies overconcern for trivial detail; more vacillation occurred over the minor decision (selecting a ring) than over the major one (selecting a wife).

When trivia triumphs

Nixon's unconscious insecurities have contributed to much of his admirable success. Having achieved almost total control over himself, he advanced to the Presidency of the United States, thereby assuming the most significant possible control of his environment. In command of himself and his government, he is able to fend off distressful unconscious feelings of helplessness and vulnerability that are ever threatening from within.

The growth of grandiosity

I will now reexamine Nixon's compulsive drive to accumulate all possible knowledge, including details. By examining the underside of all stones, he derives a security in knowing everything that can happen. He provides insurance against future uncertainties and prepares for the unknown. Ideally, the unknown becomes known; if unexpected occurrences can be eliminated, anxiety is kept under control.

Still trying to master everything

While it is obviously impossible for anyone to master all knowledge, Nixon has an inclination to try. It gives him a subjective feeling of comfort, of preparedness. These strivings give rise to illusory feelings of omniscience. In turn, this pansophical illusion presumes uninhibited abilities or omnipotence.

I have already illustrated both sides of this axis. Nixon's quest for omniscience was apparent in his endless preparation for the Khrushchev meeting and his oversolicitation of opinion in the Hiss case. His pursuit of omnipotence was reflected in the exhaustive 1960 Presidential campaign through all fifty states, including Alaska.

In Nixon's account of that campaign he asks: "Why does a candidate add to a schedule that is already too full? Why does he exert himself to the outermost limits of mental, physical and emotional tension?"

I think the answer can be found in the distorted omnipotence of his own self-image. His perfectionistic attempts to be all-knowing (with Khrushchev) and all-powerful (with a fifty-state campaign) lead from fear of omissions to a general posture of grandeur.

By assuming this stance Nixon can see himself as superhuman and therefore not endangered by the usual threats that ordinary humans must face. In this unconscious milieu of heightened self-importance, he proves to himself and to the world that *he need not operate by the rules*. How can the usual standards apply to someone who is, by way of his overwhelming perfectionism, exempt from the laws of man and nature? The comforting illusion of grandeur tends to extend across all aspects of Nixon's functioning. And so, much as in the case of Steve Cleansman, the strivings for superexcellence grow into unconscious feelings of grandiosity, and at times they become conscious as well.

The mechanisms that turn insecurity into grandeur are not in themselves pathological. I do not mean to imply that Nixon is afflicted by "delusions of grandeur," as are patients in highly pathological mental states. The more subtle mechanisms of evolving grandeur that I have just described are almost universal. We all need to defend ourselves against anxiety, and this is one very effective way it is often done, unconsciously and consciously.

I discuss Nixon's grandiosity because it is, first of all, a very consistent component of his

Why he sees himself as superhuman

His grandiosity is consistent

personality. Second, it is one of several important Nixon characteristics that profoundly influenced the evolution of Watergate. Third, it is important to point out that, while the outgrowth of grandiosity is comforting and not in itself pathological, it does have untoward side effects.

To illustrate: Nixon recalls another major epi-crisis of the 1960 Presidential campaign—the nationally televised series of debates with John F. Kennedy.

Prior to the first debate, Nixon had been hospitalized with a severe knee infection; he was still recuperating at the time of the first telecast. His weight was down, and he continued to experience some pain from the infection site. The debate went rather poorly for Nixon, and close associates told him that he looked physically poor. In the aftermath, he explains how he could have used the excuse, "I really wasn't feeling up to par. But this simply is not the truth. I had never felt better mentally before any important appearance. . . . My knee still bothered me a bit but when I'm keyed up . . . I do not notice pain at all."

Excessive self-expectations

Nixon's last statement is probably true; when one is "keyed up," pain often glides out of awareness. But when he says that he never felt "better mentally," he is dropping a subtle hint about his superhuman self-expectations.

While admitting to some physical discomfort, he speaks in superlatives about his mental capabilities. He claims exemption for himself from the usual rules governing health; he separates his mind from his body and claims that one was functioning in a superlative fashion while the other was ailing. (I am confident that Nixon consciously believed what he said here.)

When confronted by associates about his poor general appearance, he projected some of his human limitations onto the T.V. camera: "The T.V. camera is like a microscope: it shows not how one feels but what his physical condition actually is."

The TV camera "lied"

For the most part the camera was focused on Nixon's face. Whatever it showed must have been a reflection of facial expression—i.e., how Nixon felt totally, mentally and physically. Yet he denies the objectivity of the camera and the eyes of his colleagues in favor of his own subjective feeling of omnipotence. Nixon goes on to deny this reality in detail; he places the blame on his low weight, as evidenced by a loose-fitting collar, etc.

At another point in the campaign we again

"Proof" of infallibility

see a tired Nixon, convinced of his superhuman ability and displaying a need to deny human limitations. Prior to making a particular speech, he underscores the driving necessity to expose no weakness: "I don't know when I have ever felt so weak before walking out onto a public platform but I was determined to let no one know my condition." As proof of his infallibility, he continues with a comment on how some reporters labeled it "my best speech of the campaign."

He is really saying that if anyone had somehow learned of his "condition," his own illusion of omnipotence would have shattered. Nixon would then have become susceptible to the (to him) intolerable insecurities that go along with being human.

Anonymity is vital

Grandiosity also dictates anonymity. To maintain itself, no one must be allowed to know what is going on inside. The submarine must not be allowed to surface.

Nixon's third crisis was President Eisenhower's heart attack, which occurred while Richard Nixon was Vice-President. In the aftermath of the President's hospitalization,

Nixon felt it was important for him to keep a low profile so as to discourage the public from looking upon him as an ambitious opportunist.

At the outset he redemonstrated the usual excessive concern over avoidance of mistakes. After being told in a definitive way of Eisenhower's diagnosis, Nixon insisted that "Doctors can make mistakes. I don't think we should announce it as a heart attack until we are absolutely sure. . . ." He was then reassured that the doctors *were* absolutely sure; in this case it was Nixon who was becoming unsure.

Now his unconscious sphere of grandeur was threatened. He began to fear that others would read his mind. The result was his insistence that he hold no press conference. But even this much anonymity was not enough; Nixon's deep-seated fears of exposure needed still more protection—remember that the submarine must not be allowed to surface:

A fear of having his mind read

". . . We agreed that it was vitally important that I not only have no press conference that evening, but that I avoid being pho-tographed. . . . Even a camera can misquote or misinterpret a man. An unconscious, uninten-tional upturning of the lips can appear in a picture as a smile at so grave a moment. On the other hand, too serious an expression could create an impression of fear and concern which would also be most unfortunate."

A most revealing statement

This most revealing statement is evidence of phenomenal unconscious fears and desires that are threatening to break through the surface into consciousness. These fears and desires are alien to Nixon's awareness. Any human being in Nixon's position (a Vice-President who might be replacing a President) would have to be experiencing an uncomfortable admixture of feelings:

1. Nixon must have felt genuine regret for the ailing President who had chosen him as a running mate.
2. In another sense, Nixon would understandably experience some fear of the possibly impending awesome responsibilities.
3. The idea of becoming President (aside from the unfortunate circumstance making it possible) must have been enticing.

Fear was inadmissible

Among these feelings of understandable ambivalence, only number one could have been considered appropriate for deliberate, public expression. It is Nixon's grandiose stance that made numbers two and three such overwhelming threats. He could not admit to himself the reality of being merely human, and therefore fearful as well as excited in this most eventful situation.

His need to deny these characteristically human thoughts pushed them out of awareness (repression). These thoughts (operating from the unconscious) now showed themselves in disguise; this accounts for the highly exaggerated fear of being photographed. In expressing misgivings that the camera can "misquote or misinterpret," he seems to be demonstrating a fear that his *unconscious impulses* would be "quoted" or "interpreted."

In this crisis he expressed his grandiosity in another way, too. He overrated his importance by assuming that monumental outcomes would result from his actions. When Nixon comments that "too serious an expression could create an impression of fear and concern which would also be most unfortunate," he implies something rather dramatic. He was concerned that if a newspaper photograph interpreted fear on his countenance the country would perhaps have gone into a state of panic. He

Grandiose concern over a photo

exaggerated the consequences of even the most transient facial expression.

Perhaps a more succinct example of this aspect of heightened self-importance came in the wake of Nixon's sixth crisis, his defeat by Kennedy. In discussing the need to be diplomatic in defeat he says, "I would try to conduct myself in such a way that even those who had been most bitterly opposed to me would find nothing to criticize." He goes on to say eventually: ". . . it was important now with so many eyes so sharply focused on me that, from a purely personal standpoint, I try to set a proper example of conduct in defeat."

A distorted belief that critics can be soothed

This demonstrates his own sense of distorted omnipotence in two ways. First, he expresses the belief that he can act so as to soothe even his most avid critics. This is highly unrealistic thinking for a seasoned political veteran. Second, he emphasizes his exaggerated sense of self-importance in stressing how "so many eyes" would now be focused on *him*. (One need only recall Nixon's defeat of George McGovern to realize how rapidly the loser falls out of the public eye. Ironically, Nixon felt that in *his* defeat he would be closely scrutinized.) More absurd is the feeling of importance that Nixon places on himself as the defeated candidate. In point of fact, his feelings of grandeur protect him from the reality that now the "eyes" will be focused on Kennedy.

Finally, Nixon's grandiosity is also illustrated by what *Fortune* magazine (October 1973) calls his "imperial life style."

The "imperial life style"

While no recent American president has been lacking in luxury, Nixon extended the personal perquisites of the nation's chief executive to an unprecedented degree. In the process, he exhibited an intense desire to acquire not only extreme privacy for working and living but to create almost surrealistic buffers to place between himself and the vast mass of mere mortals.

When it comes to the President's personal working environment, *Fortune* describes this flight from humanity as follows:

Nixon's penchant for solitude has resulted in an unparalleled proliferation of offices. Soon after his election, he concluded that the Oval Office was too formal and had a complete office installed in the next-door Executive Office Building. Later he had additional equipment put into the Lincoln Study at the White House to enable him to work there. Nor was the

Nine private offices

President content with the existing office in Camp David's Aspen lodge. He had a second one set up in another lodge—a sort of hideaway within a hideaway.

Since then an office has been installed in his Key Biscayne home, another at Robert H. Abplanalp's house on Grand Cay, and two in San Clemente. The official western office is in the million-dollar working complex. And a second-floor den in the San Clemente mansion was converted into Nixon's ninth working office with the installation of communication equipment and some $4,800 of government-purchased furniture.

The cost of splendid isolation

To achieve the desired grandeur of splendid isolation for his living environment, Nixon required remarkable expenditures of public money, including $418,000 for a helicopter pad and $14,000 for a shark net for his Key Biscayne residence. And among the items that added up to the $6.1 million required to "secure" his San Clemente estate were the following: $13,500 for a new electric heating system, $23,000 for a sprinkler system, $53,000 for interior wiring, $130,000 for exterior wiring, $1,853 for a flagpole and another $476 to paint it.

Fortune concluded: "The attitude of the man at the top toward his perquisites is generally a reflection of his conception of his role and power. The deliberate expansion of presidential benefits tends to confirm and reinforce a monarchical vision of the office."

I fully agree that Nixon lives such a vision. A footnote to this vision is the Presidential habit of maintaining wood-burning fireplaces in all his (air-conditioned) offices, even in the summer. Only grandiosity can explain such a determined effort, in effect, to doubly defy the natural climate; to repeal the elements; perhaps even to deny that it is summer.

How to repeal the weather

5

Watergate:

An Inevitable Evolution

Given critical amounts of sunlight, moisture, gravity, chemical elements, temperature, and time, the evolution of life becomes a certainty. Given our constitutional form of government and the personality dynamics of Richard Milhous Nixon, the evolution of the Watergate operation was equally inevitable.

The "Watergate operation" refers to the entire panorama of unusual and illegal activity emanating and/or controlled from the White House by Nixon and his staff. While this section deals with a variety of activities and a multitude of personnel, it departs only slightly from the general theme of this book. For by analyzing the Watergate scandal, a great deal is

A closer look at Nixon's mind

159

learned about Richard Nixon's mental processes. Regardless of his detailed involvement or noninvolvement in the operation, his handling of this albatross has at times allowed the observer a closer look than could have been achieved at any other time.

Specifically, the efforts of Archibald Cox (the dismissed special federal prosecutor) and Senator Sam Ervin (Chairman of the Senate Select Committee on Campaign Activities) chipped away at Nixon's shield of grandiosity, thereby providing a more direct view of Nixon's inner workings.

Fresh understandings

Similarly, brief studies of H. R. Haldeman, John N. Mitchell, John Ehrlichman, and others will provide additional new insights and augment the credibility of previous insights. With the Watergate scandal as a backdrop, we will acquire fresh psychological understandings of Nixon, the man in the forefront.

The converse is also true: By examining Nixon's psychological make-up, it becomes apparent why Watergate was a process of natural evolution—inevitable. This secondary benefit of the Nixon profile will, I think, prove to be important and novel.

In this section I will attempt, therefore, to interpret the development of the Watergate activities in conjunction with the already outlined dynamics of Richard Nixon's personality. My goal is to shed significant light on both Nixon and Watergate.

I will not present a reaccounting of the Watergate events. Rather, I intend to analyze particular fundamental aspects of the phenomenon that appear to have undeniable correlations with Richard Nixon's personality dynamics. Beyond this, legitimate causes and effects will become visible.

Correlating Watergate with Nixon's personality

This section will be organized according to certain important events that followed the Watergate Hotel break-in. The details have been gathered mostly from televised testimony of the Senate Select Committee Hearings on Campaign Activities. I have also drawn from newspapers and television news accounts and numerous issues of the news magazines *Time* and *Newsweek.*

In the summer of 1971 Richard Nixon called for the formation of a special-investigations unit which has come to be known as "the Plumbers." This rather innovative nickname for the group was appropriate to the unit's operations—the name was coined to describe its

Genesis: the plumbers

function of plugging leaks of confidential White House information to the press. On the other hand, the designation "Plumbers" falls altogether short of doing justice to the delicate responsibilities of the special unit's obligations.

"Plumbers" is, of course, a euphemism. Through testimony before the Senate the activities of this special-investigations unit have been enumerated. I will concern myself only with an abbreviated list:

1. Tapping the telephones of newsmen.
2. Burglary of the office of Lewis Fielding, M.D. (Daniel Ellsberg's psychiatrist).
3. Investigation of Senator Edward Kennedy's famous accident at Chappaquiddick.
4. Fabrication of a State Department cable which would serve as an embarrassment to the late President Kennedy's administration. (The cable links that administration with the assassination of President Diem of South Vietnam.)

An extension of omniscience   I will not delve into other Plumbers' activities, in order to avoid redundancy.

Nixon's very edict to form the Plumbers unit is an extension of his own need for omniscience. Recalling that his psychological security thrives on knowing as much as possible about everything, the organization of the Plumbers can be interpreted as merely another mechanism for acquiring knowledge (intelligence). This takes on special personal psychological significance for Nixon when one considers that other established federal agencies exist which function in intelligence gathering—notably the Central Intelligence Agency, the Federal Bureau of Investigation, the Internal Revenue Service, and the National Security Agency.

Why direct control was required

Not only does Nixon need to have an inordinate amount and variety of private intelligence; he also requires *direct control* over the intelligence gathering. This explains the need to form a group apart from the well-organized, established federal intelligence agencies, and with an autonomy of its own. It is undeniable that the modest number of Plumbers could not compete with the FBI or CIA in a thorough intelligence-gathering operation of sizable scope. But the Plumbers were not established because of any incompetence on the part of existing agencies. They were established because, unlike the FBI or CIA, Nixon could maintain total direct and indirect control of their operations.

The small White House intelligence unit was a personal intelligence unit to meet the personal needs of its founder—an inevitable extension of Nixon's psychological need to have total control over himself and his environment.

The tiny elite group could have been better named "The Agency for the Maintenance of Personal Omniscience." It gathered information because intelligence-gathering decreases anxiety in the face of the otherwise unknown and puts Nixon in a unique position of power.

Why reporters' phones had to be tapped

The tapping of newsmen's telephones satisfies Nixon's appetite for omniscience in more than one way. By obtaining information through this route, he can "psych out" his enemy. To Nixon, the press, like the Communists, are looked upon with fear and assigned the status of enemies.

This attitude is based on Nixon's need to "shut the world out." The job of the newsman conflicts with his need. The reporter's job is to gather *his* own kind of intelligence. When this intelligence involves Nixon's activities, the well-fortified Presidential shell of anonymity is painfully threatened.

I think Nixon's fear of the press is constant but fluctuating. (One index of his relative feelings of insecurity before the press might be his avoidance of using a podium during press conferences, as has been suggested by journalists.) With the evolution of Watergate, there was a reappearance of the podium.

The podium as a fortress

Anyone who has done any public speaking is aware of the added feeling of security that a podium provides. While Nixon used to pride himself on standing directly before his audiences, he began using a podium again in the wake of his administration scandals.

Viewing the situation in this light, the wiretapping of a reporter's telephone can be regarded as a Presidential counterintelligence or counter-"psyching" operation. This fits in with Nixon's distorted apprehensions over the role of press coverage and helps to explain why the man demonstrates so much contempt for the press. I alluded to this Nixonian preoccupation earlier when I described his inappropriate fear of the television camera during the Kennedy-Nixon debates, and the photographer's lens in the aftermath of President Eisenhower's heart attack. Nixon's ultimate fear of the media is grounded in the danger that they will somehow get a glimpse of

Counter-"psyching" the press

what is happening in Nixon's mind.

The fear of reporters, television cameras, and photographers has a significant parallel: The same psychological constructs explain Nixon's vexation with psychiatrists. We need only exchange the camera and its film for the psychiatrist's eyes, ears, and brain. Nixon views the psychiatrist's mind in much the same way he considers the camera lens or the reporter's pen.

A dread of mind reading

Nixon feels that in some way the psychiatrist will read his mind and possibly expose him for what he dreads he might be. To a certain extent, all of these fears are predicated on reality; I point them out because, in the context of his personality, Nixon greatly exaggerates these qualms.

Consequently, intelligence operations aimed at newsmen become a psychological weapon of defense. By gaining intelligence over a press correspondent, Nixon feels he is less at the mercy of his enemy, because intelligence equals power.

Accordingly, one purpose of a tap on a newsman's phone is to find out what the newsman actually knows about Nixon (counterintelligence). This enables Nixon to monitor closely and constantly the degree to which his protective shell is being penetrated. He can then fortify any weakness before things get *out of control.* The aim of the game is to maintain, or rather keep from losing, control. The Plumbers' activities acted as a monitoring device to allow Nixon to continually evaluate the effectiveness of his own control systems.

Equally important is another apparent benefit of the newsmen telephone taps. It stands to reason that among the monitored communications, some material was beyond the realm of news. A multitude of personal conversations (e.g., between a newsman and his wife) must have been recorded unbeknownst to the unsuspecting victims. The gathering of such personal intelligence takes on a different kind of meaning. Initially intended to serve a defensive and protective function, intelligence gathering now takes on an offensive form. Through the "submarine effect" mechanisms, knowledge of the personal aspects of newsmen's conversations contributes to Nixon's general position of power. Just like such agencies as the CIA and the FBI, Nixon fully realizes that intelligence equals power.

Telephone taps mean power

Considering Nixon's dread of psychiatrists, the break-in into Dr. Fielding's office takes on additional meanings. Though it is known that

Breaking into the psychiatrist's office

Nixon set up the Plumbers operation, it is not known whether he himself ordered (or had advance knowledge of) the psychiatrist's office break-in. But I do not require the direct answer to that puzzle in order to arrive at the following deduction.

In the light of Nixon's televised Watergate speech of August 15, 1973, I can trace the President's attitude toward the burglary of Ellsberg's psychiatrist's office. One must assume from the care with which that speech was written—there were eleven drafts—that the effort to achieve a particular effect was most deliberate throughout. A section from that speech indicates that, regardless of Nixon's involvement or noninvolvement in the actual burglary, he must in any event condone it, if not secretly applaud it.

A curious omission   In defending his refusal to release the secret White House tapes as evidence, he compared his demand for secrecy to the confidentiality that protects communications in other professions. Specifically, he cited as a parallel the confidential relationship between "a lawyer and a client, between a priest and a penitent, and between a husband and a wife." As I watched the live broadcast, I was immediately struck by the obviously deliberate omission of "doctor and patient."°

By this omission Nixon tells us a great deal about himself. As a lawyer, Nixon is surely not alone in lacking respect for the confidential relationship between a doctor and his patient. But I suspect that this lack of respect is especially pronounced for Nixon in the case of a doctor specializing in the practice of psychiatry.

Nixon, like the many other lawyers who were caught in administration scandals, endowed his own profession, law, with his own grandiosity. Because *he* is a lawyer, he places great emphasis on the importance of that profession; so in his own profession strict respect for privacy must be tolerated. But he scoffs at the suggestion of a similar privilege for a doctor and his patient; that relationship does not in his own mind enjoy the immunity that derives from grandiosity.

The special grandiosity of some lawyers

Furthermore, where the doctor is a psychiatrist, Nixon probably visualizes that professional as a two-edged sword. The psychiatrist is

°I recall that Dan Rather of CBS, one of the most consistently perceptive newscasters I have seen, was also impressed by the conspicuous deletion, and said so in his post-speech analysis.

someone who is to be feared (as described earlier) but who is also to be taken advantage of, as in the Ellsberg case. In the White House obsession with psychiatric intelligence, the psychiatrist is relegated to the role of an intelligence machine.

Too close a look   Again, Nixon's fear, contempt, and exploitation of the psychiatrist is a reflection of the same personality mechanisms that make him fearful and contemptuous of the press—all these objects of his fear threaten to look at him too closely.

The fact that the Plumbers made an illegal entry into a psychiatrist's office attests to their confidence in this professional's ability to "read minds." Such confidence in a psychiatrist may or may not be exaggerated, depending on the individual case, but it is this very confidence in "mind-reading" abilities that makes Nixon so afraid and contemptuous.

Once again, the "submarine effect" is of integral importance in this connection. Theoretically, by gaining intelligence into the mind of Daniel Ellsberg, Nixon could assume some power over this long-time critic of his. And Nixon's definite hatred of Ellsberg becomes apparent when one considers why Ellsberg was placed on trial in the first place. By making the

Pentagon Papers public, Ellsberg was poking a hole in the well-fortified governmental wall of secrecy surrounding the gathering of domestic intelligence. This was tantamount to an intolerable penetration of Nixon's own shell of secrecy and grandiosity, particularly since the Pentagon Papers reflected adversely on the administration's war policy. (I note this not to condone or condemn Ellsberg but to point up another psychological parallel.)

The Watergate Hotel break-in itself became historically important only because it was detected and therefore initiated the complex sequence of events that followed. Again, I am obviously in no position to know what, if any, specific degree of guilt is attributable to Nixon personally. However, a break-in into the opposition headquarters reflects a general Nixon theme. **Degree of direct involvement is academic**

In this case the enemy was the Democratic National Party. If an effort to become all-knowing about Democratic activity could be successful, then enemy power would be defused. The question of Nixon's degree of direct involvement becomes academic in this psychological study.

The same personality mechanisms stimulated Nixon to overprepare for the Khrushchev meeting in Moscow. The applicable principle is to know as much as possible about the enemy to insure the desired future outcome and ward off future anxieties. In the Khrushchev meeting it was necessary for Nixon to appear in a good light while jousting with his enemy. In the Watergate break-in it was necessary to gather intelligence to help insure the election outcome.

More and more overkill   This theme of overkill applies in the Ellsberg case, too: Everything must be done (regardless of legalities) to insure the "right" outcome. *"Overkill" is a theme woven throughout the fabric of Watergate and the life of Richard Nixon.* Its aim is to insure absolute control over the future whenever possible and at all costs.

The Chappaquiddick investigation was yet another means of gaining an advantage over an "enemy" by knowing everything possible about him. By gaining this upper hand of omniscience, one can probe for weak spots whenever the necessity arises. This is almost a paraphrase of numerous Nixon statements in *Six Crises.* In the case of the Nixon investigation into Senator Kennedy's bridge accident, the aim could only have been to stockpile ammunition *now* for a possible future emergency—e.g., Edward Kennedy's Presidential nomination. (The trumped-up State Department cable, also apparently aimed at the Kennedys, will be discussed later.)

Inescapably, the advent of the Plumbers unit was a direct outcry stimulated by Richard Nixon's central personality functions as described in previous sections. Earlier I described a variety of *internal* control mechanisms developed by Nixon to fend off anxiety. The Plumbers unit was an analogous *external* control mechanism. It filled the same function: to fortify Nixon's internal sense of security and power by promoting omniscience. This leads to a feeling of omnipotence and a comforting psychological illusion of grandeur.

The plumbers fostered an illusion

This can be reiterated by paraphrasing Leon Salzman: There is a strong need for guaranteed avoidance of anxiety that one refuses to acknowledge consciously. Acquiring intelligence and an appreciation of the weaknesses of other people is essential. The complex strivings of some people demand intelligence and a skilled understanding into the workings of society and the weaknesses of other men.

Because I will refer again to Nixon's "illusions of grandeur," it is important for me to be precise in my use of this phrase. An illusion is a misperception of something; for example, an optical illusion occurs when an observer misperceives something that he is looking at. When I speak of Nixon's "illusions of grandeur" I refer to the man's misperception of his own gradations of greatness.

By this I mean that he looks upon himself as **But no** being more important and almighty than he is **delusions** in reality. This is not to be confused with a "delusion of grandeur," which is defined as a fixed false belief. Delusions of grandeur are seen in psychotic individuals who, for example, believe they are someone other than themselves. A most common example of this is the psychotic person who believes that he is Jesus Christ.

In general, the presence of delusional thinking indicates the presence of significant mental illness. While this is not the case for illusional thinking, Nixon's apparent illusions of himself certainly suggest at least the presence of a personality problem.

The fourth Plumbers activity that I listed was the creation of a counterfeit cable designed to embarrass the administration of John Kennedy. From Senate Committee testimony, it is known that the text of the phony cable links the assassination of South Vietnam's President

Diem with the late President Kennedy's administration.

To appreciate the critical psychological ramifications of such a ploy, it is once more helpful to remember Steve Cleansman. Steve, in his self-made world of grandiosity, felt a special exemption from the general rules of society. ("He was exempt from the usual rules and regulations of society and marched to his own drumming.") It is this crucial principle that sanctions the Diem cable fabrication. It also sanctions other illegality. In a word: The Plumbers group, created by Nixon and supervised by chief domestic advisor John Ehrlichman, brought to its assignments a collective air of grandiosity and arrogance which exempted them from etiquette, law, or general respect for human freedoms.

Sanctioning the counterfeit cable

This is most delicate territory. The Plumbers, according to testimony, were created by Nixon, supervised by Ehrlichman, held accountable to Egil (Bud) Krogh, and engineered by E. Howard Hunt and G. Gordon Liddy. The collective psychological aspects of their behavior resemble those of Steve Cleansman. I make this comparison to achieve clarity and to avoid accusing Richard Nixon directly.

Again: it is not my purpose to pass judgment

He set the tone for the plumbers on Nixon's degree of involvement. But I must point out that the psychodynamics of the Plumbers activities mesh faithfully with the dynamics of Nixon. I therefore conclude that, Nixon having created the unit, his personality structure and his personal example must at least have set the tone for the Plumbers' work. Certainly it made the Plumbers feel important and legitimized.

In psychiatry one often speaks of activities that are "ego-syntonic" or "ego-dystonic." Ego-syntonic activity goes along with the general grain of one's personality (e.g., a gangland executioner finds murder ego-syntonic). Ego-dystonic behavior is the converse (e.g., a man reasonably happy with his marriage of ten years flies off the handle while intoxicated, murders his wife—and is immediately remorseful).

My point is that, irrespective of Nixon's degree of involvement, the activities of the Plumbers were, in my opinion, ego-syntonic for Nixon. His subsequent apparent remorse over the scope of the Watergate "caper" and other activities is probably unrelated to his purported disapproval of them. His sadness can be better explained by his anger over the fact that the operations were exposed.

I can say this with confidence in view of material to be presented in the last chapter. Nixon's grandiosity and consequent feelings of exemption (and his insistence on executive privilege and immunity) make all these dismal happenings ego-syntonic. The basis of his sadness over being exposed most likely resides in a psychologically significant loss. For exposure was more than a politically embarrassing defeat. It meant the intolerable: loss of control. It provided the public with a guided tour of the Executive Branch as operated by Nixon, including a view of secret operations. Given Nixon's obsession for secrecy, the Watergate affair must be an ultimate nightmare for this man.

Why exposure was intolerable

There is at least one direct example of Nixon's ego-syntonicity (approval) for the illegal Watergate activities: Nixon's known involvement in the Pentagon Papers trial of Daniel Ellsberg.

The Judge Byrne fiasco

A long-time critic of Nixon's Vietnam war policy (and, ironically, a former consultant to Henry Kissinger), Ellsberg was being prosecuted for his part in making secret Pentagon documents public. Through John Ehrlichman

Nixon offered Judge Matthew Byrne, who was presiding over the Ellsberg case, the directorship of the FBI. In the advanced stages of that case Ehrlichman as well as Nixon himself met with the Judge about the enticing FBI job plum.

Ellsberg equals Alger Hiss

The Ellsberg Pentagon Papers episode had been an appalling embarrassment for Nixon's tight executive-military operations. Nixon must have equated Ellsberg with such people as Alger Hiss—the enemy within who must be eradicated.

In the Alger Hiss case, Nixon's asset was his anxiety-driven quest for knowledge. It proved to be productive indeed: His scrutiny of detail in that investigation definitely paid off. But that was 1948. Although he worked hard even then to make himself all-knowing, he was only a freshman congressman. In 1973 we see Nixon not as an omniscient congressman but as a grandiose President. Claiming special exemption for himself, he is able through ego-syntonicity to commit an improper act. As an article in *Time* (August 20, 1973) pointed out, if Nixon were a private citizen he could be prosecuted for having tampered with the judicial process when he offered Judge Byrne the FBI job while the Ellsberg trial was in progress. But Nixon obviously felt himself untouchable by the rules that govern mere mortals.

Nixon's personality structure can be seen operating in an infinite variety of ways throughout the Watergate scandal. The aspects that have already been described are again summed up well by Salzman, who was writing long before Watergate and not in relation to Richard Nixon.

Untouchable and untouched

The nature of this kind of personality is to strive for compulsivity and perfectionism. It reaches for omniscience and omnipotence in order to insure its very existence. With success, the grandiosity expands and remains untouched even when failure occurs. "It leads him to view himself as exempt from natural causes and events and permits him to engage in the most extreme and arrogant kinds of behavior."

Although Salzman was not talking about Richard Nixon, I believe he was describing Nixon's personality pattern in a nutshell.

In the wake of the Watergate break-in, several of Nixon's external control mechanisms can be seen to have crumbled. One of the greatest losses was the forced resignation of

Licking the wounds of Watergate

aides H. R. Haldeman and John Ehrlichman. (Their White House roles will be discussed later.) With his most trusted inner staff in almost total collapse, Nixon was left stripped of many strongholds of external protection. This left him more vulnerable and allowed closer, more reliable observations into the Presidential psychology.

Increased vulnerability dictated that Nixon regroup some of his already established psychological defenses. Salzman, again writing prior to Watergate and without Nixon in mind, in effect summarizes Nixon's post-Watergate psychological stance:

"He invariably overestimates his cunning and underestimates the capacity of the police **"Immunity ...** and others. Most of his failures arise out of **exemption ...** foolish and arrogant errors...." Moreoever **privilege"** there "is a grandiose presumption of immunity and a certainty of exemption and privilege...." Such persons "are always surprised, annoyed, and disappointed when caught. They insist that the incident was an accident."

This statement describes the attitudes and behavior of Nixon and/or the Watergate conspirators in both a specific and a general way. Amazing in its accuracy and applicability, it is a mind-boggling diagnosis, considering that it was not meant to describe anyone in particular. The familiar ring of Salzman's statement arises out of the fact that he is referring to a very particular personality pattern familiar to psychiatrists. Nixon seems to fall into that same general pattern.

(I am avoiding the use of diagnostic labels until the very end to avoid leading the reader away from general perspectives. Labels serve mostly to abbreviate one's thinking. Furthermore, unless one fully understands the meaning of a label it will only lead to confusion and confinement of thought.)

In Nixon's post-Watergate behavior the "grandiose presumption of immunity" emerged during his earliest dealings with Senator Sam Ervin's Select Committee on Campaign Activities. Nixon's omnipotent psychological stance led him to forbid his aides to testify publicly, under oath. **A highly threatened personality**

This is not merely a President invoking his appropriate legal powers. This is an inwardly insecure (and now highly threatened) personality, attempting to protect itself with consoling, illusory grandiosity.

Again, it is worth recalling Salzman's diagnosis that the psychological mechanism which results in grandiosity leads a person to feel "a certainty of exemption and privilege." Nixon's claims of executive privilege for his entire staff were not founded on legal grounds. Such naiveté on his part could be puzzling when one considers the man's deserved reputation as a competent lawyer. It can only be explained by the fact that the claims for special privileges were not based on Nixon's legal knowledge. They were rooted in his psychic grandiosity.

"Executive poppycock"

The first part of my last statement is supported by the view of another lawyer, Senator Sam Ervin, who said: "That is not Executive privilege. It is Executive poppycock."

It is not my intention to set up a picture of a good guy against a bad guy. I am simply trying to document that ffixon's claims in this instance are not legally based, but psychologically based. It recalls the Nixonian obsession to maintain control—in this case unrealistic control—over his entire staff.

The Nixon tapes: recorded reiteration of the Nixon profile

As the Watergate scandal blossomed, it became possible to see Nixon's complex series of external psychological defense mechanisms first boldly exposed and then stripped away. A classic example is that of the famous White House tapes.

Among the most startling testimony before the Senate Select Committee was the soberly spoken revelation of a former minor White House functionary, Alexander P. Butterfield. A one-time aide to H. R. Haldeman, Butterfield, who was by then employed in private industry, straightforwardly described how Nixon had directed the Secret Service to install voice-recording equipment in Nixon's Oval Office, his Executive Office Building office, and the Cabinet room. (After Butterfield's disclosure, Nixon said he ordered the equipment's removal.)

This reiterates and adds credibility to much of my theoretical foundation of Nixon's psychiatric profile.

First we must examine Nixon's own professed motives for establishing the elaborate system of eavesdropping. He and his aides claimed that these recording devices were to preserve a running account of all oral communications for the sake of history. Even if we were to accept this at face value, Nixon is confirming personality characteristics that I have previously discussed. This is especially true since Nixon has an excellent memory that

No fragment must be lost

surely will serve him well in writing his own memoirs. But he is again preoccupied with *all* detail and shows a fear of leaving *something* out. It is not enough for him to rely on his excellent memory and his Presidential papers to recall important details of conversations. It might even be dangerous. Certainly the prospect of losing some fragment of some conversation feels threatening to him.

The inevitable hundreds of thousands of feet of recording tape would be almost impossible to edit. If transcribed, they would surely fill the shelves of a library. Can so many utterings from one person, even a President, be of that much importance? To Nixon, esconced in the milieu of his own grandiosity, the answer is definitely in the affirmative. The preoccupation with the permanent recording of every minuscule detail is paramount to a personality that fears leaving anything out. The open-ended, almost infinite gathering and mechanical memorizing of conversations represents the pinnacle of omniscience.

Up periscope The now familiar "submarine effect" also comes into play with the Nixon tapes. Recalling this integral mechanism of his personality, we can see what was probably Nixon's *primary* motivation in setting up his office as a recording studio. We can apply my analogy of Nixon as a submerged submarine captain whose periscope makes him aware of all that is going on about him, including all conversations.

Personally, the submarine captain (Nixon) is anonymous with respect to the tape recorder. I mean that he knows it is there; consequently, by controlling his candor in the recorder's presence, he enjoys selected anonymity.

Being aware of this unusual setup, Nixon gained a sense of power over anyone with whom he spoke in his office. Since the purpose of the recorder was to record "history," Nixon was able to speak selectively with his victimized guests and edit himself so as to place himself in a favorable light vis-à-vis the microphone. *His ultimate goal is to control history.*

How to control history

And so our master of total command is not only concerned with controlling his present and future. He even organized a system to control his past-to-be.

The periscope analogy is so valid here that one need only change the medium from sight to sound. This yields more than analogy; now we have actuality. Guided by Nixon's knowledge of the recorder and his victim's ignorance of the machine, Nixon alone could always show his best side to the microphone. Like a periscope, the microphone became a one-way valve that put only Nixon's unsuspecting conversational partners in a bad light.

Only guests were on "Candid Camera"

Knowledge of being filmed or taped always affects one's performance, usually by restraining one's candor. In this way, Nixon's office recording of history became a contriving of his own conduct for the sake of history; for his recorded office guests it was like being on *Candid Camera*.

It is most important for Nixon to see himself in a good light, which the tapes certainly enabled him to do. This is the most dramatic example I can think of to demonstrate the use of omniscience by Nixon to place himself in a relative position of power over others—indeed, over the whole world. For the use of the tapes could assure him of several truly Orwellian powers:

1. Omniscience—no detail of any conversation could ever be missed.
2. Omnipotence—proof would always be available (to Nixon only) to protect himself if necessary. This use was demonstrated when Nixon lent tapes to H. R.

Haldeman to defend the administration against the Senate Select Committee on Campaign Activities.

3. Grandeur—Nixon's place in history as a "good" President could be written (contrived) ahead of time by Nixon himself. He could write his own history by manipulating crucial conversations in his favor. In this way Nixon's excessive control even encompasses his own immortality.

In view of the psychological ramifications, I wonder whether the taped "evidence" really has any credibility. At the time of this writing the struggle between Nixon and the forces of Archibald Cox and Sam Ervin over the use of the tapes as evidence is yet unresolved. In view of Nixon's control over the recording sessions, the control over the tapes themselves seems to me an academic legal point. For, whether or not the tapes are released, Nixon will retain the original control of the material on those tapes that he established in the first place.

Nixon's conditional release of the tapes seemed to me still another example of his need to stay in control. By giving up the tapes he

Nixon exercised control from the start

could avoid having to submit to an all but inevitable Supreme Court ruling to surrender them. So in the end it was Nixon—not the Court—who controlled the fate of the tapes.

The return of Frank Nixon: pneumonia, summer 1973

I preface this section by admitting that I must engage in a certain amount of speculation regarding the physical-medical background of Nixon's hospitalization for viral pneumonia. But the crucial psychodynamics that I can describe are far above the realm of speculation in the context of Richard Nixon's past history.

I do not include this section to sensationalize or to theorize on the possible cause and effect of Nixon's malady. But one cannot responsibly overlook the probable ramifications evidenced by the timing and secondary benefits of Nixon's hospitalization. My purpose is to define and describe an important psychological conflict that arose out of the Senate investigation and its connection with Nixon's conscious and unconscious memories of his father.

The stress was overwhelming

In light of the detailed account I have presented of Nixon's personality characteristics, it is plain that his illness occurred at a time of (and probably because of) *overwhelming* psychological stress. Two overriding factors are

of special importance in considering the onset
of Nixon's hospitalization.

1. A great deal of Nixon's psychological
   security as a conpetent person depends
   heavily on his ability to maintain control
   of all situations affecting him.
2. Nixon has a tremendous revulsion of submission and fear of authority—traceable
   to childhood dealings with his father and
   other figures of authority.

Just prior to being hospitalized with virus-
caused pneumonia, Nixon agreed to have a
meeting with Senator Sam Ervin to discuss the
President's refusal to release White House
evidence to the Senate Select Committee. For a
period of several months Ervin had represented
Nixon's chief challenge in the Watergate scandal.

In psychiatry one often speaks of a
psychological construct, originally postulated
by Freud, known as "transference." Tech-
nically it is a "mechanism by which a person
reacts to someone as if he were a significant
figure in the individual's past, usually a parent"

**Nixon's
transference
reaction**

(*Psychiatry*, Eaton and Peterson). One of my teachers defines it more simply as a case of mistaken identity. When someone reacts to another person as though he were a parent, we say he is experiencing a transference reaction.

It is my opinion, from all accounts and observations, that throughout the months of the Watergate scandal Nixon experienced and suffered the effects of a transference reaction with Sam Ervin.

How can I say this?

First of all, Ervin is a seventy-six-year-old man whose looks alone are those of a wise old father; Nixon, at age sixty, is young enough to be Senator Ervin's son. Almost anyone might in some ways react to Ervin as a father. The general respect he demands and receives attests to this. As Senate Majority Leader Mike Mansfield said: "Sam is the only man we could have picked on either side who would have the respect of the Senate as a whole." The very name Sam Ervin rings synonymous with authority.

While these Ervin characteristics are most obvious and of some significance, they are the least important regarding Nixon personally.

Nixon: "A naughty son" Being older than (and unafraid of) Nixon, Ervin's condescensions and irritations have placed Nixon in the role of a naughty son.

While Nixon holds the highest office in the government, he finds, ironically, that Ervin has, in the eyes of many, somehow achieved even higher status. Neil MacNeil of *Time* states this in a cogent way: "Sam Ervin has been called 'the last of the founding fathers'—and in a way it's true."

More ominous must be the threat Nixon perceives in the Senator: the man's omniscience in the field of Constitutional Law. Reputed as the Senate's foremost authority on this subject, *he threatens Nixon with Nixon's own familiar weapon: total knowledge.*

Ervin has been described by journalists as having, in a sense, prepared for this battle throughout his life. Even when compared to Nixon's tendency to overkill, Ervin's preparation seems to eclipse Nixon's efforts to defend himself.

And so, not only is Ervin older than Nixon, he is better prepared and just as aggressive. He poses the greatest psychological threat to Richard Nixon, the menace of stripping away the many layers of Nixon's protective shell. And inside is an insecure, submissive boy who dreads being exposed. **A better prepared enemy**

Sam Ervin, like Frank Nixon, is a man "never to be argued with." Nixon surely sees Ervin as he saw his father; he must have a relentless dread of this exhumed specter of his father, and it must haunt him unmercifully.

Like father, like scandal This becomes even more plausible when we recall Frank Nixon's outrage over the Teapot Dome scandal—specifically, his disgust over President Harding and his corrupt administration. Now it is Frank Nixon, poorly disguised as Sam Ervin, who is outraged over President Nixon and *his* corrupted administration.

In many ways these analogies bridge the gap between the two father figures and again become realities. Both on an unconscious and conscious level, Nixon must constantly feel reminded by Ervin of his angry, authoritarian father. But now his image of a father is outraged at his son. The reawakening of repressed unconscious fears in Nixon's mind are indisputable.

The dreaded reunion Considering the preceding transference dynamics, it is evident that Nixon's impending meeting with Sam Ervin was psychologically equivalent to reuniting with an outraged father. The anticipation of this meeting must have been intolerable to Nixon, who tends to have difficulties with face-to-face discussions anyway, and much prefers solitary deliberations. I feel that the phenomenal psychological stress could very well have provided a basis for the pneumonia.

What linkage exists between stress and a virus infection?

Viral pneumonia rarely occurs in healthy people, except when physiological resistance is lowered. It is a relatively common complication of cancer and other chronic debilitating diseases. Nixon has been a generally very healthy President, in a physical as well as a mental sense; he seems to pass his routine physicals with ease. Assuming all of the medical reports were accurate, there would be no question that an infection with a respiratory virus was the immediate cause of Nixon's illness. I am suggesting that Nixon might well have been made vulnerable to the infection by considerable psychophysiologic (psychosomatic) stress.

Looking for the "stress organ"

To add further possible credence to my postulation, it is worthwhile to mention the concept of the "stress organ." In many people with well-established psychophysiologic illnesses, stress is most likely to manifest itself in one particular organ. For example, the chronic ulcer patient can expect stomach pain when under stress.

To my knowledge, Nixon does not have any

well-established site of psychosomatic illness (stress organ). But some considerations of his past medical history and family history should at least be considered.

Target: the lungs

As I mentioned earlier, Nixon as a child almost died of pneumonia, and has a family history of tuberculosis. Though this is necessarily speculative on my part, some evidence points to a stress-organ system—the lungs. But once more I emphasize that the dynamics of Nixon's transference reaction with Sam Ervin are paramount. The psychosomatic considerations of his pneumonia are interesting, but I present them primarily to help describe the intensity of the transference.

Summarizing the psychology of Watergate

Focusing on the Watergate events in general, their overall theme was to gain absolute control over all aspects of the election; not to help win a victory for Richard Nixon, but absolutely to guarantee it.

The efforts to take command of the election amounted to dramatic overcontrol, beginning with the primaries. The general strategy was to knock Edmund Muskie out of contention for the Democratic nomination and to guarantee a convention victory for George McGovern. The mechanisms of control were to break through the normal political limits and permeate the inner workings of the opposition party. Once McGovern was nominated the mechanisms of overkill became even more evident, as the unfolding Watergate affair made all too plain to anyone capable of watching television.

Few knowledgeable people seemed to feel that McGovern could win the election, even by a long shot. Nevertheless, the undaunted Committee to Re-Elect the President continued to labor, devising more and more "dirty tricks" to nail down a Nixon victory.

More and more "dirty tricks"

I cannot help thinking that Nixon's own unconscious lack of confidence in himself had an indirect and a direct effect on the principles used by the Committee to Re-Elect the President. His own self-uncertainty (which was evidently shared by his own committee) probably accounted for the omission of Nixon's name from the name of the Committee itself. The decision to avoid naming the organization "The Committee to Re-Elect Richard Nixon" must have been at least okayed by Nixon, if not made by him.

Nixon finds security in remaining anonymous, even in the midst of his own guaranteed-to-succeed reelection campaign.

6

The Nixon Group

A handful of aides, close friends, and other associates constituted a most exclusive and symbiotic consortium of Nixon confidants during the period that is at issue in this book. A simplified overview of this fan club will further fill in Richard Nixon's psychiatric silhouette.

I will deal only with certain members of the small club who seem to have augmented Nixon's previously established personality mechanisms. As in the Watergate chapter, I will hopefully provide in this section a secondary benefit: limited insights into the psychological workings of the club membership itself.

At the outset I want to stress that the few

The symbiotic relationships relationships that I examine in these pages are psychologically symbiotic. That is, the various club members filled in by making up for some of Nixon's psychological weaknesses, and vice versa. These personalities were more than associates: They were additional extrinsic psychological mechanisms of defense for the President.

The occupational breakdown of these Nixonites forms a wider spectrum than does the psychodynamic breakdown. We find John Ehrlichman, former attorney and advance man; John Mitchell, attorney; H. R. Haldeman, former ad man; Billy Graham, evangelist; Spiro T. Agnew, former Governor of Maryland; Charles (Bebe) Rebozo, real-estate speculator; and Robert Abplanalp, inventor-millionaire. (For reasons that will become apparent later, I have deliberately excluded John Dean, Henry Kissinger, and others inextricably linked with Nixon.)

Aside from personal and professional involvements with the President, the men that I discuss share a commonality in the part they play in the maintenance of Nixon's psychic integrity. In other ways they also share some common personality characteristics; for Richard Nixon, it appears that like charges attract.

Despite his once grand governmental responsibilities, the public has been allowed little direct insight into the working and thinking of H. R. Haldeman. The candid, personal-sounding "Bob" nickname becomes a non sequitur when attached to this man's calculating demeanor. Paradoxically, though, he appears to me to be the most predictable and easiest to understand of the Nixon inner circle. I shall set aside more space for him than for most of the other members, and for good reason.

H. R. (Bob) Haldeman: the protector

First of all, he seems to have been the most powerful man in the White House, after Nixon. Secondly, despite significant outward dissimilarities, Haldeman's underlying personality mechanisms seem to be almost identical to Nixon's.

Over and above the remaining members of the club elite, Haldeman served as an impressive reinforcement for Nixon's protection against underlying insecurities. In return for this important service, Haldeman was rewarded with the job that best facilitated the continued rendering of this service for the President. At the same time (and symbiotically), the job, White House Chief of Staff,

Why he got the job

satisfied Haldeman's own psychological appetite.

Ascending from the status of a Los Angeles ad man to Washington White House Chief of Staff is an unlikely, if not absurd, climb. But I believe that it is anything but absurd. Haldeman was not chosen for the high position because of his vocational qualifications. He was chosen for an infinitely more compelling reason: a deep psychological need on Nixon's part.

"Buried in a 1959 time capsule"   Some significant characteristics could be deduced about this former Presidential aide just by observing his appearance. It was almost as though he had been buried in a 1959 time capsule, only to be exhumed for a nostalgic look at that period. His hairstyle could easily pass the most stringent of Marine dress codes; of greater importance, it reflects his need for military-style organization and uniformity.

Evans and Novak report: "Early in 1969, Haldeman ordered all White House male personnel to wear ties and jackets at all times while at work—an edict producing concealed hilarity and massive disobedience; the order was quietly forgotten."

Cleancut meant antiseptic   The flattop that would have rendered him anonymous fifteen years ago ironically made him conspicuous at the White House—indeed, it became his trademark. His suits tended to be gray and muted, with thin lapels; his general appearance was clean and ultraconservative. It is not so much that H. R. Haldeman is cleancut: He is antiseptic.

The bland look is an apparent reflection of his own meticulously guarded personality mechanics. Like Nixon, nothing is likely to be more important to this man than the absolute avoidance of losing control. He differs in this respect from Nixon only in the way he manifests his preoccupation for total command of himself and others. Nixon controls via *obsession* with knowledge, which leads to omniscience; Haldeman controls more through *compulsivity,* by keeping things carefully organized and neat.

Well-suited for his job of controlling the staff, he ran a meticulously organized, efficient White House, down to the most minute of details—witness his failed attempt to establish a dress code. His own office, like his appearance, was immaculate.

Compulsivity (Haldeman), like obsession for detail (Nixon), ideally leads to a feeling of security through being in control. By having everything carefully organized and in its

Knowing "where" meant knowing "what"

proper place, one need not have anxiety over it. Having things in order is tantamount to having them in control. Knowing *where* everything is becomes equivalent to knowing *what* everything is.

Nixon and Haldeman have very similar psychological dynamics; they merely use different means to accomplish the same thing—containment of anxiety by control of self and environment.

The complementary personality dynamics of these two men allow them to support one another. Nixon looks to Haldeman for external psychological supports, which, like the flying buttresses of Notre Dame, bolster from without. Haldeman receives reciprocal benefits from Nixon.

The "ship" was a fortress   During his years in the White House, H. R. Haldeman quickly earned a reputation for running a "tight ship." The "ship" could better be characterized as an impenetrable fortress; it was commonly referred to as the "Berlin Wall," erected and patrolled with the aid of John Ehrlichman. In this way he and Nixon served as buttresses for each other.

Haldeman essentially served as another external control mechanism for Nixon, by guarding him from unwanted visitors. Just as the

Secret Service bodyguards protected Nixon's physical integrity, Haldeman protected the President's emotional integrity; he was like a "Secret Service" *mental* guardian.

The July 30, 1973, issue of *Time* said: "Haldeman was first among equals, the dour watchdog at the Oval Office gates who determined who and what the President saw and heard." In the context of my submarine analogy, Haldeman, in this role, acted as a bulkhead for Nixon.

"Mr. Bulkhead"

He also served as a kind of hatchet man for Nixon; he could execute necessary face-to-face confrontations with people in situations that would have devastated Nixon. For example, it was Haldeman who played a decisive role in dissolving the staff of Interior Secretary Walter Hickel following the Secretary's own precipitous departure.

Evans and Novak report: ". . . the true key to the inevitability of Haldeman may be best explained in the personality differences between him and the President. Haldeman, crew cut and unsmiling, had a most un-Nixonian ability to demolish an aide, a colleague or an outsider with harsh word and icy stare."

Like Nixon, Haldeman was grandiose with

"A member of the family" power, probably because of similar personality dynamics. This too is supported by *Time:* "In his zeal for absolute power, Haldeman even tried to replace the President's personal secretary, Rose Mary Woods, who has been at Nixon's right hand since 1951, and is almost a member of the Nixon family."

For Haldeman, the need to control is an overriding factor in life, a preoccupation. Not only does this man thrive by exercising absolute command of himself, including his emotional feelings; he must control others. Because Nixon's personality shares the obsession, it becomes obvious that Haldeman was ideally suited to function as Nixon's protector.

Billy Graham: the chaplain While H. R. Haldeman was probably the most supportive outside influence for President Nixon's psychological structure, Billy Graham was probably the most perverse. I see him as the "Chaplain" of the Nixon inner circle; certainly he represents the religious stance of the more important club members, as well as Nixon himself. We know that Nixon was the product of a "bible pounding" Methodist father and a staunch Quaker mother. Haldeman and Ehrlichman are Christian Scientists who dis-

dain (and abstain from) liquor and tobacco.
Graham, the ultimate world figurehead of
Protestant fundamentalism, began his relationship with Nixon in the early 1950s. One
might classify him as the fundamentalist's fundamentalist.

Some analysis of paradoxical religious fundamentalism explains Nixon's gravitation
toward religious people, who either practice
this brand of religion or are the product of such
backgrounds. I have placed great emphasis on
Nixon's need to keep from losing control; it is
not a coincidence that these religious per-
suasions are likewise obsessed with controlling
rules and regulations. To be a good fundamentalist one must strive for total self-control. The
reward for this is total self-righteousness.

Fundamentalists strive for total self-control

Starting with numerous "Thou shalt nots,"
these forms of obsessional religion preoccupy
themselves with the stringent regulation of
sexual mores, dress, social habits (e.g., drinking
and smoking), crime and punishment.

Regarding the last, the fundamentalists place
great stress on the eye-for-an-eye concept and
on misguided threats of hell. Their outlook on
life is one of self-righteousness; endurance of
temptation is considered most virtuous. Their
outlook on outsiders is one of contempt; they

cast a punitive eye at those who do not live up to their rigid outlook and those who commit evil.

Hateful impulses are attached to others

Employing the mechanisms of repression and projection (see "Nixon the Anti-Communist"), they do not recognize many of their own hateful and aggressive impulses. These impulses are projected outward and attached to others: sinners, Communists, etc.

Their strivings for (illusory) self-righteousness lead to grandiose feelings which sometimes allow a person to feel exempt from the usual rules of society. These ramifications again are reminiscent of Richard Nixon's own modus operandi. And so it is that, while they are able to scrutinize and castigate others for misdoing, they often conveniently overlook their own misdoings.°

Billy Graham: advance man

Billy Graham is the inevitable religious symbol of the Madison Avenue-oriented Nixon administration. Just as Haldeman and Ehrlichman were experienced "advance men" in previous political campaigns, Billy Graham is his own advance man. An acquaintance of mine put it aptly: "Billy Graham is a metaphysical used-

°It is interesting, but not surprising, that fundamentalists account for more than their expected statistical share of impulsive homicides.

car salesman." He fits the Nixon inner circle like a glove because of the religious dynamics that he represents and exploits.

His climb to international prominence, like Nixon's, was in the Horatio Alger mold: He began as a Fuller Brush man. I have observed Graham closely and with great interest for several years, and feel confident that he too shares many of Nixon's personality traits:

Another Horatio Alger

1. He is inwardly (unconsciously) insecure.
2. He is obsessed with controlling himself and others.
3. Unconsciously, he is powerfully aggressive and even hostile.
4. He uses massive amounts of projection to relieve his tremendous unconscious storehouse of hostilities. The hostilities are tacked onto a variety of scapegoats, mainly "nonbelievers" and Communists.
5. Graham is grandiose and intoxicated by as well as addicted to power.

Those characteristics are demonstrated every time he preaches. It would take another book to document this analysis fully, but my personal observations of Graham bear out these findings dramatically.

A famous slip   One of Graham's most famous slips of the tongue occurred during one of his crusades when he advocated castration as a punishment for rapists. According to *Time* (April 16, 1973), "Graham acknowledged that his statement was 'an offhand, hasty, spontaneous remark' that he immediately regretted."

His underlying punitive aggressions came to the surface spontaneously in this illustrative instance. William Sheridan *(Technocratic Trendevents,* August 1973) concludes:

Graham's slick marketing of religion has become another big business, and his "anticommunistic" moralizing fits in well with his good friend Nixon's political efforts. . . . Beneath the public image of piety which Graham and his "crusade team" have created with all of the madison Avenue techniques available, there lie some startling tendencies. Graham advocated a second invasion of Cuba; he considers most of the ghetto flare-ups of recent years to be communist inspired; he permits his organization to be used for C.I.A. operations when in foreign countries.

Graham, like many of his counterparts, is

contemptuous and condescending toward those who are less perfect and omnipotent than himself. In this way he becomes a symbol, an example for such men as Haldeman and Ehrlichman. His attitude toward rapists can be equated with Nixon's view on capital punishment for murderers.

An example for the omnipotent

Nixon, in fact, has long based his reputation on the illusion that he, too, is a crusader against evil. He has long been identified as such: a rabid anticommunist, aggressive congressional investigator, promoter of law and order (outside the White House), and, at least in lip service, avid eradicator of cancer.

Ultimately it becomes clear that Billy Graham is another external support to Nixon's personality structure. This symbiosis operates in at least three ways:

1. Graham provides a moral stamp of approval that encourages Nixon (in the name of God) to strive for *control* of those things that *he* (Nixon) arbitrarily defines as evil (e.g., pornography and abortion). As before, the key concept is *control*. Graham facilitates Nixon's use of the psychological mechanism of projection. That is, Nixon can derive comfort from Graham's spiritually sanctioned scapegoating.

The Billy Graham symbiosis

2. The contrived sacred aura of Graham and his old-time religion tends to make some of

Nixon's policies sacrosanct. Nixon can feel (e.g., in his advocation of capital punishment) that, like Moses, he is acting in the name of God. This makes it more difficult for the opposition, who must penetrate this grandiose alliance with the heavens.

Invoking the emotions
3. Graham, like Haldeman, possesses a personality characteristic that complements a Nixon personality deficit: Graham has infectious charisma. He can reach people on an *emotional* level with Nixon-style policies and philosophies. This sweep of emotional inspiration is totally foreign to Nixon's outer personality structure.

Construct number three gives rise to a perverted form of nationalism, which I will term "Nixonalism." Nixon policy and attitude, when backed by Graham's influential spiritual leadership, take on an almost metaphysical quality of sacredness. When Nixon waves away an enemy (e.g., a Senate dove) for being unpatriotic, the put-down is ex cathedra. Nixonalism (Nixon = the nation) makes Billy Graham, more than any other person on the current scene, responsible for promoting this brand of superpatriotism. He adds a touch of Gospel to what Nixon says, thereby rendering Nixon's words unquestionable.

And so, just as Haldeman served Nixon as an

external controller, Billy Graham serves as an appendage of charisma and promoter of grandeur.

John D. Ehrlichman, like Graham and Haldeman, resembles Nixon somewhat in personality dynamics. But more important, Nixon's top domestic-affairs man augments certain aspects of Nixon's psychological structure. I refer primarily to two related Nixon characteristics: grandiosity and the consequent exemption from the usual standards by which people must operate.

John D. Ehrlichman: Knight in tainted armor

Ehrlichman fully accepted the premise of Richard Nixon's grandeur and therefore aided Nixon in holding on to this anxiety-relieving illusion. The July 30, 1973, issue of *Time* reported: "Ehrlichman once told a reporter: 'The President *is* the Government.'" In this instance illusion borders on delusion.

The Ehrlichman testimony before the Senate Select Committee showed his own brand of grandiosity. If we recall the concept of ego-syntonic versus ego-dystonic behavior, it is safe to say that it is an ego-syntonic activity for Ehrlichman to take a casual view of illegalities. To take such a view of such acts does not seem to go against the grain of his personality.

Wrongdoing was no problem

This is explained by a sense of superhumanness that Ehrlichman shared with his leader. Here is the paradox of a man who abstains from the "evils" of drinking and smoking but condones the investigation of political candidates to uncover *their* drinking and sexual practices. This is probably made possible by the dynamics of his religious fundamentalism; he can derive from it a feeling of self-righteousness (by not drinking).

The immunity of the self-right-eous This same self-righteousness augments the grandiosity that allows him to be casual about burglary, bribery, and many other improprieties. An August 6, 1973, *Time* article comments on Ehrlichman's brilliantly evasive testimony: "In his chilling concept, it does not matter that there is both a law and an ethic to protect every man's conversations. . . . If Government wants it, there ought to be a way to get it. After all, insurance adjusters, any private detective, seem to find a way to bribe a nurse or pose as a doctor. Why not the White House?"

Considering Ehrlichman's statement that "The President *is* the Government," he is really saying that, in his state of grandeur, Nixon is above all the laws of mankind and any act of this supramortal is justified. And so Ehrlichman personally elevates Nixon's status to that of king—and his own status to that of knight.

Placing Billy Graham in the position of archbishop, one begins to visualize an awesome chess game. But the analogy sadly falls apart. There are no players; the pieces move about the board autonomously and unopposed until the game is up.

Spiro T. Agnew, from the time of his unexpected initiation into the Nixon Club until his forced resignation, was always considered a junior member. His insatiable hunger for money and power have been testified to by his recently exposed financial track record as a Baltimore County official, as Maryland's Governor, and as Vice-President. His evasion of income taxes reflects the now familiar theme of special exemption arising out of grandiosity. On the Nixon chessboard he was but a pawn, expended quickly and with minimal ceremony.

Spiro T. Agnew: offensive lineman

I include him mainly to point out his important psychological function as another appendage of Nixon. Compulsively clean in grooming and tall in stature, he served as a spokesman for Nixon in areas not cultivated by the fearful President. It was Nixon's gigantic fear of the press that Agnew could effectively and vicariously quell. His speech in Des Moines, Iowa (when he castigated the New York-based television network news departments), must have given Nixon a feeling of vicarious power comparable only to another Nixon spectator favorite—football.

The surrogate football player

In his youth, Nixon was a mediocre football player; his prominence as the nation's number one football fan probably relates to surrogate feelings of accomplishment that he can feel when rooting for his favorite team and advising his favorite coach.

Watching Agnew assault the press, a chore at which Nixon is also mediocre, must certainly fulfill for the President, by way of a substitute, the psychological need to conquer this enemy.

Picking Agnew for what he wasn't

In addition to Agnew's function as an antagonist to the press, he fulfilled other Nixonian psychological needs. Since Nixon has always been so obsessively thorough in his preparation for events and decisions, one might be surprised at how he could have picked a running mate with a closet full of skeletons. I think the answer to this puzzle lies in the fact that Nixon probably chose Agnew for what he *was not*, rather than for what he *was*.

Richard Nixon, living in his self-made euphoric world of grandeur, probably *could not have conceived of being replaced—whether by disability, death, or impeachment.*

After all, part of grandiosity is an assumption of immortality. In the light of this assumed uniqueness, I do not think Nixon viewed a Vice-President in his administration to be of any importance or even of potential importance. And in the event that something happened to Nixon, he could still have some reassurance in knowing that the country would miss him in the presence of Agnew, a third-rate hypothetical President.

In some ways Nixon recapitulated the pattern once again in picking Agnew's successor, Gerald Ford. While Ford seems to be a man of established integrity, he grossly lacks any kind of national charisma. An undying congressional supporter of Nixon, Ford seems to be yet another appendage to the President.

Repeating the pattern with Gerald Ford

Despite the enormous influence that John N. Mitchell has had on Richard Nixon and his career, I will not dwell on him because the Mitchell-Nixon interrelationship seems to have been less symbiotic than the other relationships I have described. It seems that John Mitchell, former Nixon law partner and Attorney General, was his own man. His psychological relationship with Nixon does not seem to demonstrate the psycho-interdependencies of Nixon's relationship with Graham and others.

But in another sense Mitchell had a sig-

John N. Mitchell et al.

nificant psychological impact on Nixon. Nixon looked up to Mitchell as the powerful, decisive, seemingly unflappable man that he was until the time of his downfall. These were characteristics that Nixon never seemed to feel were a part of himself. Similarly, Nixon marvels at such business successes as Charles (Bebe) Rebozo and Robert Abplanalp.

Identifying with "success"   Both, like Mitchell, represent identifications of success. Nixon needs to cling to this kind of identification because he was deprived of it as a child; his father was never financially powerful. Other authors who have written about Nixon's links with these men describe their dealings as father-son relationships, especially when it comes to the handling of money.

Other men, such as Henry Kissinger and William Rogers, have also played important roles in Nixon's present and past, respectively, but these relationships, too, do not seem to be predicated on psychological symbiosis. Others on the endless list of "Watergate characters"—John W. Dean, III, Charles Colson, etc. —are also of importance to Nixon, but not in the same psychological sense as Haldeman et al. Many psychological parallels exist to varying degrees between Nixon and these men, but further analysis would only reveal a redundancy of patterns.

7

Diagnostic Impressions

Throughout this book I have detailed what I feel to be the crucial psychodynamics that constitute Richard M. Nixon's psychiatric profile. In doing so there is little question that a particular, complicated but well defined set of mechanisms emerged. They tend to fall into an area suggestive of the classification *obsessive-compulsive personality*.

The American Psychiatric Association *Diagnostic and Statistical Manual* defines the obsessive-compulsive personality as follows: "This behavior pattern is characterized by excessive concern with conformity and adherence to standards of conscience. Consequently, individuals in this group may be rigid, over-inhibited, over-conscientious, over-dutiful, and unable to relax easily."

Defining the "compulsive obsessive personality"

221

This definition, while accurate, is incomplete. The psychodynamics described in the Steve Cleansman chapter more completely describe this type of personality. The outward characteristics of this personality (overinhibition, compulsivity, overconscientiousness, and strivings for perfection) are all mechanisms used by the obsessive-compulsive. These mechanisms are used by such a person to gain control over himself and his environment. In this way, he will not lose control of himself —and his environment will not be able to control him.

Anxiety is the fuel

This series of mechanisms is fueled by anxiety, which constantly threatens to overwhelm. The omniscience, omnipotence, and grandiosity tend to be the inevitable offshoots of the obsessive-compulsive's unrelenting strivings for total control. All of these very complicated mechanisms seem to fit the personality characteristics of Richard Milhous Nixon.

Of greater importance, I hope I have given understandable insights into the causes and effects of Richard Nixon. Such an understanding is essential to an understanding of 1973, perhaps the most bizarre political year in American history.

Is Nixon "Dangerous"?

While I have expressed the opinion that Richard Nixon tends to display "obsessive-compulsive" personality traits, and that he does not suffer from mental illness, this does not answer a variety of inevitable remaining questions:

What is my overall impression of his emotional stability?

Three key questions

How would Nixon tend to act in the midst of a grave international crisis, especially a massive attack on the United States?

How might this man deal with a poor outcome of the extensive investigations into his administration's corruption or the bizarre financial manipulations involving his two luxurious estates?

225

Keep an eye on that temper

Regarding Nixon's emotional stability, he can be characterized as overly stable, if not rigid, most of the time. Over the years this has given him an image of substantiality. In contrast, I remind the reader of the man's highly explosive temper. I have traced this back at least as far as his boyhood, when he released onto brother Donald a year's supply of anger and hostilities.

More recently, the public could see Nixon's volatility surface prior to a long-awaited Watergate press conference, when he angrily and roughly shoved press secretary Ronald Ziegler. During that press conference his voice was often heard to quiver. At times he seemed unable to control the modulation of his speech. In some instances his syntax was jumbled, reflecting momentary periods of confusion. His facial expression showed stress, and his body posturing was highly mechanical even by Nixon's robotized standard. It was after this press conference that many observers expressed concern over the President's general condition.

A hazardous side effect

This brings to mind a possibly hazardous side effect of Nixon's tendency to overcontrol himself. Such necessity for total command is not conducive to the venting of anxiety and anger when, as, and if these emotions arise. Instead, they are forced to rise to the surface in the form of volatile outbursts and impulsive reactions. His famous 1962 remark to the press, "You won't have Dick Nixon to kick around," is a verbal equivalent of the Ziegler shove.

I have presented only a few examples of the Nixon pattern, but in view of the biographies it is a well-established one. It is this pattern of overcontrol alternating with volatility that gives me some feelings of uneasiness about the man.

He seems to allow himself too little oppor- **Unpredict-** tunity for emotional release of anger and anx- **ability in an** iety; such releases are more likely to come out **international** all at once. If this should occur in the midst of a **crisis** great world crisis, a Nixonian outburst could have far-reaching, possibly even catastrophic consequences. If one adds to this his impulsivity in decision making, Nixon emerges from this profile as a highly unpredictable man.

More succinctly stated: Emotionally, Nixon is highly organized and stable. In fact, he tends to strive toward overstability (rigidity), which makes him fall prey to explosiveness in the midst of a threat.

But another great paradox surfaces. In the **When Nixon** midst of the most ominous kind of crisis, such as **would function** a foreign invasion of the United States, I think **well**

Nixon would function well and for good reason. Such a disaster would tend greatly to enhance Nixon's responsibilities, and, thereby, the feelings of psychological grandeur that bring him so much comfort.

So in all probability his comfort and confidence would increase in the context of his own realistically elevated importance. My theory is supported by a remission in Nixon's drawn physical appearance that occurred with the onset of the Middle East fighting of October 1973. As he states over and over again in *Six Crises, he acts best in crisis.*

I would amend this to include *only non-personal crises.* In other words, I think the threat of world war poses less of a vexation for Nixon than the outcome of Watergate, San Clemente, and other personal scandals.

To be watched: A personal crisis

It is in this personal context that I am most concerned about Nixon's stability under stress. A very bad outcome to his personal campaign financing, the investigation of his income taxes, or the San Clemente/Key Biscayne scandal might prove to be disastrous to the man.

And so, in the context of a national emergency I think I might sleep well knowing that Nixon is awake and at the helm. But in the midst of the various personal scandals that have been plaguing Nixon, I think he has shown significant amounts of strain already.

To document my picture of a Nixon functioning well in an international crisis, as opposed to a shaky Nixon in personal crisis, I point to the Vietnam war. In his numerous dealings with the press and television about the handling of that war, he appeared relatively confident and in command. This is explained by the fact that he was dealing with an enemy far removed and onto whom he could project his own inner aggressions. Despite protest marches and other demonstrations, his own personal integrity was not at stake, as it was in the revelations of administration corruption.

What Vietnam showed in Nixon

On the eve of the would-be meeting with Sam Ervin (see the Watergate chapter), Nixon's own personality shell was made vulnerable, and the resulting stress seemed greater than the Vietnam war stress even though the latter involved the life and death of millions of human beings.

Even more ominous, though, were the developments of October 20, 1973, the day Nixon fired special Watergate prosecutor Archibald Cox. This led indirectly to other firings and resignations, including that of Attorney General Elliot Richardson. In the after-

The bizarre firing of Archibald Cox

math of this sudden shakeup, Nixon went so far as to order the prosecutor's offices to be sealed off. Here Nixon's overriding fear of exposure, combined with his grandiosity, apparently gave rise to incredible impulsivity in his actions.

The series of bizarre events was the inevitable result of Cox's unrelenting demands for the famous White House tapes. This would-be invasion of Nixon's shell of secrecy seemed to have become overwhelmingly stressful for this man who demands so much control.

Going beyond the "normal"   Such stress was shown by Nixon during his erratic press conference of October 26, 1973, when he viciously assaulted the electronic media. In the midst of his intolerable personal crisis, Nixon's illusions of grandeur begin to resemble more-fixed beliefs; at least momentarily, he seems to be taking on the identity of an all-powerful monarch.

It seems to me that on this occasion Nixon at least temporarily went beyond the limits of behavior that we label with the admittedly difficult-to-define word "normal."

So my major concern would be about any hypothetical situation in which Nixon was greatly threatened on both levels, personal and international. Such a dual crisis could present risks.

In no way is this book meant to be a diatribe against Richard Nixon. I have not been concerned as much with his strengths and weaknesses as I have been with presenting an overall personality picture. One conclusion that must be realized is that Nixon is indeed human—albeit with some reluctance on his part. In the midst of his Presidential aura and grandeur, many lose sight of this undeniable fact.

Uses and abuses of psychiatric profiles

I want to caution the reader about the potential misuse of psychiatric information and opinion. During the 1964 Presidential campaign between President Lyndon Johnson and Senator Barry Goldwater, the American Psychiatric Association, through a reckless questionnaire that was sent to its members, declared by majority opinion that Goldwater was unfit as a Presidential candidate. While insight into a candidate's psychiatric status is every bit as valid as an appraisal of his cardiac status, the asinine APA fiasco was inexcusable. In actuality it amounted to little more than an inventory of psychiatric political opinion. Goldwater was a victim of leftward-leaning psychiatrists passing instantaneous judgments on a rightward-leaning candidate.

An ill-founded appraisal

Having lived in Arizona for several years, I have seen a great deal of Goldwater through the local news media. I have even had occasion to correspond with the man. I do not have as much insight into Goldwater's inner life as I now do into Nixon's, but from my exposure to Goldwater I have come to believe that the majority of my APA colleagues of 1964 knew very little about this man in general, and less about his mental status in particular. Their collective response to the misguided questionnaire was therefore most probably a reflection of political judgment, not psychiatric judgment. I feel confident that the negative psychiatric appraisal of this man was ill-founded. To my knowledge, there is no reason to think that Goldwater's mental state is abnormal.

Because of the inaccuracy and inevitable harm of such questionnaires, I think they should be curtailed. To make a valid psychiatric assumption in absentia on a political figure, the man's past and present must be researched. Because I *have* researched Nixon in a variety of ways, I feel that my profile of him takes on more validity than the results of any would-be Nixon questionnaire.

Another question regarding psychiatric

profiles should be dealt with: What about the routine use of psychiatric examinations of candidates for high public office? I see no reason why the examination of a candidate's psychiatric status should be considered of any less importance than an electrocardiogram, X rays, and a physical examination. The latter are routinely done, and the results are routinely made public. It is absurd to think that a political figure's mental status is any less important than the status of his physical health. Had this procedure been carried out, the fateful and abortive Thomas Eagleton Vice-Presidential candidacy might have been avoided.

Psychiatric examinations for political candidates

In view of the widespread scandals that permeate Richard Nixon's administration, it is reasonable to inquire whether these developments might have been prevented.

The psychiatrist as a barometer?

I think there is little question that the President's personality dynamics set the stage for the Watergate dynamics. Whether a psychiatric profile several years ago would have provided any preventive medicine for the scandalous political year of 1973, I honestly cannot say. But it appears clear that if the results of such an examination had been made available to the voters, Nixon could not have abused his Presidential grandiosity as he did. The man on the street, guided by such a profile, might have seen through the President's cries of "national security" and "patriotism," which at times have served as an ironclad Nixonian protection from dissent.

What about suicide?   Regarding such risks as the possibility of Nixon committing suicide or suffering a psychotic breakdown, the psychiatrist is of less help than one might expect. It is one matter to evaluate a man's mental status at a given time; it is quite another matter to predict his future.

In retrospect, Watergate seems to have been an inevitable outgrowth of Nixon's personality, yet an actual forecast of Watergate would not have been possible. The reason is simple: Much of what has been deduced here about Richard Nixon could only have been validated in the context of his scandals—after the fact.

9

The Need For Psychiatric Profiles:

An Evaluation
by Louis L. Bruno, M.D.

I have on occasion wondered why a President is necessary. I see myself, perhaps naively, as a rather liberal, well-educated young man of the twentieth century. As a psychiatrist and as the product of a healthy, intact family, I have been the fortunate recipient of a fine Eastern-Establishment education. Because I am obviously a well-qualified voter, I have often felt guilty around election time for not voting, especially in Presidential elections. But as a result of recent events and my thinking about the study in the foregoing pages, I believe that these guilt feelings, like so many other such feelings that trouble many of us, have been understandable

237

but quite unnecessary. For my apparent apathy was not apathy; it was grave concern.

"No real choice"

In the past I have rationalized my failure to exercise my franchise by deciding that there was no real choice among candidates. However, in 1972 this transparent defense of my apparent negligence was shattered by the appearance of a candidate who struck me as a mild-mannered, peaceful, sensitive, intelligent man from South Dakota. George McGovern was someone I could identify with, respect, and admire.

Embarrassingly, my voting record remained blank, increasing my remorse one-hundred fold. This uncomfortable state compelled me to try to understand why I could or would not vote. While pondering this, the realization came to me that I really did not understand for what I would be voting. Just as most people would feel uncomfortable signing a confusing legal document, I feel uneasy voting for something I do not understand, which explains my initial question: Why is the President necessary?

Is the office more important than the individual?

The President obviously serves many practical, necessary, and perhaps important functions. It would be pedantic for me to enumerate his chores. However, it seems to me (and evidently to many others) that there is a much greater significance to the Presidency. This became apparent during the Watergate hearings when man after presumably honorable man explained how he felt the office was so important that they could not only risk their future careers but bend and outright break laws they had devoted their lives to defend. Even the President himself seemed to say that the office was more important than our revered rights of the individual. This feeling about the importance of the Presidency is obviously shared by many citizens, and was strongly documented not only by the national interest in the Watergate affair but also by the hysteria surrounding the mere mention of impeachment.

The Presidency is, no doubt, of great importance. And with considerable soul searching, I came to a few personal conclusions, some of which reflect on the personalities of those men who seek high public office. First, being a liberal or conservative is only a programmed set of mind. In other words, we are conditioned to a political stand, much the same way as we are sold a new car or an in-vogue clothing style.

This becomes more evident when one considers the current trends in a candidate's repertoire: the use of television, make-up, and

Everything is "image"

public-relations men. His chances of success are measured by the way he presents himself—by his public image, rather than by his abilities, experience, or political philosophy. Nixon has so successfully utilized these techniques that it is the illusion of the man we know, not the man himself. However, I am not so convinced of Madison Avenue's power as to believe that it can create a need so universal that it touches every segment of every society that has ever existed.

To understand the need for a President, it might be useful to look at more primitive individuals and their societal needs. The saber-toothed tiger and the colossal mammoth were not what these individuals feared most—it was their unpredictable environment, the darkness, the unknown. But emotionally, the mysteries of birth and death were man's greatest threats. Even primitives sensed these threats. They represented man's own vulnerability and his own mortality.

"Existence is still the issue"

Expressed in more philosophical terms, facing the idea of his own existence and nonexistence was, and still is, man's greatest dilemma. He has built most of his institutions to alleviate this problem. Man's science, his religion, his philosophy have all in one way or another been used to cope with this dilemma. For the same reasons he has developed societies. At a fundamental stage he protected himself with walls of stone against the more immediate threats of the environment. As technology reduced these more obvious threats, it gave us the freedom to contemplate more profound issues. Yet the most significant of these issues is still existence.

On the one hand, societies were formed to help the individual deal with this question. On the other hand, the society as an entity itself must approach this problem. We know that many great societies have developed and disappeared. The reasons for these disappearances are generally not well understood. The Mayan Empire of Central and South America is a clear example of the persistence of this mystery.

A current and popular label for this very complicated concept about which I am speculating is "the existential dilemma." This is considered by many to be the "neurosis" of our time. My premise is that society itself experiences a social existential dilemma. The political system is the way that a society deals with this. The responsibility is placed in the hands of many, but especially in the hands of its leaders. It is perhaps their most oblique and

The leader's most significant duty

nebulous duty but, in my opinion, their most significant. Like the individual, society needs to define its reason for being and must defend itself against the idea of not being. Those individuals who are involved enough in their society to vote are most likely the same individuals who can identify with it. (This is analogous to the way millions of American men identify with football teams on fall weekends.) Individuals (citizens) can displace their fears and dilemmas onto society. This allows for some emotional distance, and at the same time allows one to elect a man who will promise and guarantee to protect us from uncertainty, and to define our purpose.

When Presidents put their own problems first

The best President is the man who has most effectively coped with this problem on an individual basis. Conversely, this may also give us some insight into men who seek high political office. It has been expressed many times by historians, biographers, and political scientists that our last two Presidents have had a strong need to establish themselves as great and famous leaders—to develop continuing accomplishments that would leave their names and ideas engraved on the history of mankind. In a sense, they would thereby establish their own immortality and eradicate their fear of nonexistence.

Problems arise because each man resolves his individual dilemma in his own unique way. One may become a religious zealot; another may explore areas of great social change; still another may emphasize technological and economic advances. Some unfortunately have rationalized that they were above the common man and hence invulnerable to his ultimate fate. This has led to catastrophes: disregard for the rights of the individual, corruption, and immorality. One need not search far to recall a leader who denied his mortality. Adolf Hitler's own psychodynamics affected his approach to the position for which his society had chosen him.

In general, an individual's psychological development dictates his mechanisms of coping with anxiety or discomfort. The unknown and the misunderstood phenomena, especially those affecting one's emotional and physical integrity, may leave one very uncomfortable. In other words, the realization of our own ever-impending nonexistence (and the consequent need to define our existence) creates anxiety. We develop defense mechanisms to

When defense mechanisms count most

relieve ourselves of this discomfort. This does not generally become an issue of public concern except in two eventualities:

1. if the individual's defense mechanisms are a threat to himself or others.
2. if that person is selected for possible political office.

It is this latter condition that concerns us here.

Getting insight before voting

I feel it is not only the right but perhaps the responsibility of every citizen to have some insight into the man for whom he is voting. This, I think, demonstrates the need for psychiatric study. I do not regard this type of study as a precise predictive barometer or as a scientific device to differentiate between candidates. It is a tool to help us understand where we have been, where we are, where we are going, and a way to avoid placing our trust in politicians about whose inner lives we know little or nothing.

Bibliography

American Psychiatric Association. *Diagnostic and Statistical Manual of Mental Disorders.* Washington, D.C.: American Psychiatric Association, 1968.

De Toledano, Ralph. *One Man Alone: Richard Nixon.* New York: Funk and Wagnalls, 1969.

Eaton, Merrill T., Jr., M.D., and Peterson, Margaret H., M.D. *Psychiatry.* Flushing, New York: Medical Examination Publishing Company, Inc., 1967.

Evans, Rowland, Jr., and Novak, Robert D. *Nixon In the White House.* New York: Vintage Books, 1972.

Fortune magazine, October 1973.

Mazlish, Bruce. *In Search of Nixon.* Baltimore, Maryland: Penguin Books, 1973.

Mazo, Earl, and Hess, Stephen. *Nixon—A Political Portrait.* New York: Harper and Row, 1967.

Newsweek Magazine, July 23, 1973.

Nixon, Richard M. *Six Crises.* New York: Pyramid Publications, Inc., 1968.

Salzman, Leon, M.D. *The Obsessive Personality.* New York: Science House, 1968.

Sheridan, William. *Technocratic Trendevents,* August 1973, Vol. 24, No. 277. Long Beach, California.

Time Magazine, issues March 1973–October 1973.